BETTY TOMPKINS

MO.CO. JBE BOOKS

RAW MATERIAL

BETTY TOMPKINS

An arts centre is not meant to accept the history of art as a fact, but rather to perceive it as a fluctuation – like the flow of a river, where certain turbulent currents return to their source, the narrative it elaborates often branches out simultaneously toward the future and the past. Rewriting, or rather *reweaving*, the scattered or missing pieces of this history is a task that MO.CO. has endeavoured to carry out since 2017. Betty Tompkins' first solo show in France (along with Marilyn Minter) thus corrects an anomaly which stems both from the *scandalous* character of her iconography and from the art world's structural misogyny.

Since the 1960s, Tompkins' painting has masterfully combined hyperrealism, abstraction, and feminism. Her *Fuck Paintings*, a series begun in 1969 showing close-ups of sexual intercourse, whose source images were drawn from pornographic magazines, were censored in France in 1973. Fellatio, kisses, genitals – the repertoire of images used by Tompkins literally siderates the viewer, and in particular, the frontal representation of female genitalia, which stands for what *cannot be looked at steadily*, as we have known since Gustave Courbet's *The Origin of the World*. Hence the stupefaction. Because she confronts us with unsettling images, and because she traps our gaze with extreme close-ups that monumentalize representation, Betty Tompkins reinvents the sublime in painting. The French philosopher Jean-François Lyotard saw this as the source of all modern painting: modernist abstraction, from Claude Monet's *Waterlilies* series to Mark Rothko or Barnett Newman, plays on the idea of "giving to see while preventing the act of seeing". And the sublime, according to him, consists in "presenting that there is an unpresentable. To make visible that there is something that can neither be seen nor made visible: this is what is at stake in modern painting". This definition is a perfect match for Tompkins' work, which positions itself within the field of the pictorial sublime in order to *demasculinize* it, to exhibit that which is unthinkable by indexing it to a female reappropriation of a woman's body and sexuality. Of course, we can speak of Betty Tompkins' work in terms of photorealism, but we must keep in mind that she focuses her images on the precise point where they float between representation and illegibility, between a recognizable figure and its dissolution into an abstract composition. In 1960s United States, her hyperrealist contemporaries painted scenes from everyday life or portraits, glorifying an iconography of the banal ushered in by pop art. They sought a certain neutrality, striving to show the world "objectively". It is not by chance that both exceptions to the rule, working at the same time, were women: Vija Celmins and Betty Tompkins. The former painted the infinitely large – the cosmos, the sea, the desert. The latter, what could be called the "smallest infinite", that is, the universal matrix, sexual desire, intercourse. Both, unlike their masculine colleagues (with the notable exception of French artist Gérard Gasioroswki), opted for black and white, deliberately doing away with the sensuality of colour; and both elaborated a pictorial strategy aiming to overwhelm and bewilder the viewer.

Tompkins would go on to use colour as a special effect, to cover up historical paintings and "fill" female figures painted by male artists with words. The series, entitled *Women Words*, underscores the concealment of the female gaze in the history of art by covering the nudes of classical art with misogynist discourse. In the wake of the #MeToo movement, Tompkins called for accounts of sexual assault or abuse, which formed the matrix of the *Apologia* series. Ever since the beginning of her career in the 1960s, Betty Tompkins has therefore slowly shifted the effect of stupefaction that makes up the core of her pictorial practice from generic images of sexual intercourse to the everyday violence of interhuman relationships.

NICOLAS BOURRIAUD

DON'T FUCK WITH BETTY TOMPKINS

ALISON M. GINGERAS

"I was an accidental dissident." A breathtaking understatement, this is how Betty Tompkins sums up her false start in the New York art world during the early 1970s. While she may not have set out to become a feminist renegade, her entire practice has been a case study in the assertion of free speech – against the pieties of government watchdogs, art-world gatekeepers and certain factions of the feminist mainstream. And while still a prolific artist who continues to push the boundaries of political correctness, Tompkins' fateful decision to appropriate hard-core pornography as her primary source material in the late 1960s turned out to be a timely and revolutionary position that simultaneously tested the limits of Constitutional First Amendment law and feminist discourse.

In 1969, she embarked on a series of photorealist works that she audaciously entitled *Fuck Paintings*. Rendered in airbrush on monumentally sized canvases, each work portrays tightly cropped scenes of heterosexual intercourse based upon her first husband's collection of explicit photographs. Over a period of five years, she made nine seven-feet-tall grisaille canvases that unapologetically depicted penetration.

"He came with the porn," Tompkins jokes, when asked about her ex-husband's contribution to her revolutionary subject matter. "What I was doing, when I look back on it, was *so* outrageous. A decade before he met me, he would see ads in the back of girlie magazines for photos. They were about 2 × 3 inches." As it was then illegal to send pornographic material using the U.S. Postal Service, her husband rented a P.O. Box in Vancouver and would drive to Canada from a small town in Washington state to procure his clandestine erotic stash. "He had to hide them in the cushions of his car crossing the border," Tompkins recalls. While such images are no longer prohibited by law, Tompkins' compositions still manage to startle. Her *Fuck Paintings* are simultaneously abstract and figurative: she transformed the graphic puncta of pornographic penetration into icons of sexual free speech.

Little could she anticipate how these paintings would become a flashpoint of the feminist "Sex Wars" that would rage throughout the 1970s and '80s and up to the present. Her *Fuck Paintings* were not specifically made to address shifting social mores towards sex, but the work was fermenting in tandem with major political and legal debates around the definition of obscenity. After numerous court rulings led to the progressive relaxation on the strictures of freedom of sexual speech in the late 1960s, the so-called "Golden Age of Porn" bloomed – a period that is often cited as beginning with the 1969 release of Andy Warhol's *Blue Movie* and continued with the widespread distribution of X-rated films such as *Deep Throat* (1972). Pornography polarized the women's movement: feminist discussions about women's sexual agency as well as polemics around pornography's inherent misogyny divided women into opposing factions. Tompkins herself didn't set out to take sides.

"At that time," she recalls, "I was totally unaware of all the prejudices in the art world towards the young and towards women." The catalyst for her subject matter came both from her boredom with the art that was being championed by New York galleries, as much as from the disgust with the blanket rejections she received from those same galleries about exhibiting her work. "Nobody even said, 'Maybe.' It was 'No!' Even the women dealers refused me." The emotion in her voice swells slightly as she reminisces, "When I questioned them, they all said, 'We don't show artists your age.' Then they would say, 'Don't come back at all, we don't show women.' It was shocking *and* it was also totally liberating." With nothing left to lose, Tompkins sat in her small bedroom-cum-studio pondering her next move. "I did not want to bore myself to death."

Before that *eureka* moment when she made the fateful leap to explicit sexual subject matter, Tompkins painted in the gestural, post-Abstract Expressionist style that dominated American postwar art. During her graduate studies, she pivoted towards figuration. Her Master's thesis, entitled "Advertising Media as a Source for Painting Iconography", featured several paintings depicting sexualized images of women. Anticipating the dramatic compositions of her mature paintings, early works such as *Swedishella* (1969) and *Blusher/Mouth* (1969) appropriated found images that objectified women's bodies. While Tompkins acknowledges the influence of Pop art on her student work and had seen the groundbreaking *Erotic Art* show at Sidney Janis in 1966 – an interesting note given the coincidental resonance of Tompkins' student works with the paintings of another maverick feminist Marjorie Strider – these early works foreshadow what would become Tompkins' radical breakthrough series.

Fuck Painting #1 took shape as she rummaged through her husband's photography collection. "I started cropping with my fingers, then I ripped up pieces of paper to find exactly what I wanted." She removed the models' faces, hands and feet, embarking on her new paintings in a humble, tiny space "about five feet wide between my bed and the wall." Using an airbrush loaded with white and black acrylic to achieve a hyper real effect, she created her first *Fuck Painting*: a seven-foot-tall horizontal canvas showing vaginal coitus with the female on top – a fitting position for Tompkins' prefiguration of sex-positive feminism. The anonymous woman's ass, ringed with dark shadows and some wisps of pubic hair, dominates the composition; the man's spread thighs, scrotum and part of his erect penis take up the bottom half of the canvas. Removing all traces of the couple's identity, rendering their flesh in gradations of grey, Tompkins bypassed the soft-core objectification of commercial erotica to focus on point-blank phallic penetration. Unfettered by the need to please other people, she began to explore the provocative iconography that became her signature preoccupation – as yet unaware of how divisive her subject matter would become.

Before Tompkins could even begin to establish herself, censorship waylaid her career. "When I moved to SoHo I was invited to be in a show, *A Flash of US Avant Garde: Realism, New Realism, Photo Realism*, in Paris at the Espace Cardin. At that point, I had been in two group shows in New York City, one at Warren Benedek Gallery and the other at Lo Giudice." Tompkins shipped *Fuck Painting #1* (1969) and *Fuck Painting #5* (1973) to Europe, only to have the work impounded on the French border on the grounds that it violated obscenity laws. Instead of basking in what should have been her breakout moment, Tompkins belatedly learned of the seizure. "I received a letter from the curator of the show, who said that my work had been stopped in Customs," she recalls. "I was really upset. I felt totally blindsided by the event." For over a year, Tompkins waged a bureaucratic battle to get her paintings returned to New York. "It felt like a decade in the analogue age," she says, though she did not take the news passively.

While the whole French affair was absolutely debilitating for Tompkins, she leveraged this negativity, transforming it into text elements that she overlaid onto figurative works in a series titled *Censored Grids*. With this collection of drawings that Tompkins embarked upon in 1974, she revisited the same pornographic imagery meticulously rendered in pencil, and then blurred out the "offending" parts with the word "censored" repeatedly drawn or stamped over the graphic genital imagery.

"It was a way to keep sane," she explains. "I was not up on any art history that had to do with censorship except maybe Courbet's painting." (Indeed, Tompkins' *Fuck Paintings* are the heir to *The Origin of the World* – the infamous 19th century oil painting of female genitalia – the ur-work of sexually explicit painting in the Western art canon.) "Basically, what I said was, *Oh you think you can censor me? I can do a better job*. I thought if I censored myself that it would have more legitimacy."

While initially deployed out of her frustration, text became a staple of Tompkins' conceptual tool kit. She would foreground language in much of her later work as a way of reclaiming even vile, misogynous or demeaning terms – most recently in the series *Women Words*, begun in 2013. In the same manner that she appropriated pre-existing photography for her *Fuck Paintings*, Tompkins culled her textual source material from an archive of over three thousand "terms for women" solicited via email. "What was really important with the first thousand *Women Words* on canvas was that none of them could be from me. The rule that I made was it had to be all given to me." Painted on monochromatic or abstract backgrounds, classic epithets such as "bitch," "slut" and "cunt", dominate this anthology of small canvases as do more trite phrases including "ball and chain" and the more imagistic "I'm going to Jackson Pollock all over her face." As the series evolved, Tompkins began transposing the words onto iconic works by male photographers, such as Helmut Newton and Richard Avedon.

But Tompkins' defiance could not be directed at antagonists she didn't even realize she had.

Feminist Exclusion

Around the same time that her work faced governmental erasure in Europe, Tompkins was subject to an even more powerful form of exclusion by women artists in her own backyard. Emboldened by the momentum of the women's liberation movement in American society at large, feminist artists' groups had mushroomed in downtown Manhattan. In Tompkins' SoHo neighbourhood, women-run collectives like the (also artist-run) A.I.R. Gallery were founded in the early 1970s to provide a platform for women who had been systematically excluded from the commercial art world – some of them, anyway. "I saw every show they put up at A.I.R...But my impression was *you're invited to show*. It was like a club," Tompkins says, remembering the cold shoulder she received from her feminist neighbours.

Unbeknownst to Tompkins, another coterie of feminist artists had banded together in solidarity over their right to make explicit erotic art. The Fight Censorship Group, founded in 1973 by artist Anita Steckel, could have been a game-changing outlet for Tompkins. Its manifesto seemed tailor-made for Tompkins' iconography and her own struggle against censors: "If the erect penis is not 'wholesome' enough to go into museums – it should not be considered wholesome enough to go into women. And if the erect penis is wholesome enough to go into women, then it is more than wholesome enough to go into the greatest art museums." Yet this bold vindication of phallic imagery would not be extended to Tompkins. While the group's invited members decried the puritanical policies of museums and asserted the right of women artists to reclaim this field of sexual representation for themselves, they simultaneously enforced a red line over the issue of pornography, claiming that all commercially produced pornography was a tool of patriarchal oppression.

"I had used [pornographic] photographs that I had not taken by myself, but altered," Tompkins says. "That was the main objection." Little did Tompkins realize that this objection was led by a fellow female artist who lived just down the street from her studio. Without knowledge of each other's practices, Joan Semmel and Betty Tompkins almost simultaneously arrived at making explicit sex paintings between 1969 and 1971. But a different kind of liberation spurred Semmel's arrival at erotic subject matter. Returning to New York after starting her career as a post-AbEx painter in Europe, Semmel experienced culture shock. "I had returned from Spain looking for the 'Sexual Revolution' and instead found sexual commercialization that mostly showed female bodies for sale."[1] In parallel to her jolting encounters with New York newstand "girlie magazines," Semmel experienced a political awakening – she began "to attend meetings of Women in the Arts, an activist network of female artists; the Art Workers' Coalition, an antiwar and artists' rights organization; and the Ad Hoc Women Artists Committee, a protest group started by women in the Art Workers' Coalition who 'were fed up with being asked to get coffee for the men.'"[2] Nearly contemporaneous to Tompkins, Semmel's first painting *Erotic Series #1* (1970-71) emerged in this highly politicized ambiance. Semmel had enrolled at Pratt University to earn her MFA as a means to become a teacher.

At grad school, she enacted a formal shift toward figuration while simultaneously engaging with this explicit sexual imagery. These first paintings deployed her spectacularly jarring sense of colour and remnants of her AbEx brushwork and applied them to scenes of heterosexual copulation. The first three paintings in the series were made from drawings inspired by Semmel's imagination

1 Joan Semmel, "A Necessary Elaboration" in *Joan Semmel: Across Five Decades* (New York: Alexander Grey Associates, 2015), p. 5.

2 Richard Meyer, "Not Me: Joan Semmel's Body of Painting" in *Solitaire: Lee Lozano, Sylvia Plimack Mangold, Joan Semmel*, (Columbus, Ohio and New Haven: Wexner Art Center and Yale University, 2008), p.114.

yet later works in the same series would be based on photographs she took of lovers *in flagrante delicto*. Using a palette ranging from cadium red to veronese green, this first erotic painting depicts a woman squatting atop of a man seated on a toilet. Rendered in loose brush strokes – in contrast to Tompkins' black-and-white photorealism – the explicit, richly hued punctum of the male figure's erect penis dominates the centre of the composition. With this painting, Semmel embarked on the explicitly sexual as her signature issue, entwining it with her burgeoning feminist political consciousness. As Semmel explained, "In the past, women's sexuality had always been used against them. I felt very strongly the sexual issue was crucial in terms of real liberation. So I started to work in the erotic theme, but I was very conscious of it being erotic from a woman's point of view, rather than from
3 what is normally a man's point of view."[3]

Point of view was everything – especially when it came to how these works were initially understood. Despite similarities in form and subject matter, an ideological gulf soon erupted separating Tompkins' *Fuck Paintings* from Semmel's *Erotic Series*. In these nearly contemporary works, both artists depict heterosexual fucking; both artists graphically depict genitalia – placing the erect male member at the center of their compositions. Both artists were engaging with existing cultural paradigms of heterosexual erotics. As such, Tompkins' and Semmel's turn to erotic subject matter coincided with a wave of radical feminist discourse from 1968 to the mid 1970s that addressed what activists termed, "the meaning of sexual pleasure for women in a patriarchal society. Ti-Grace Atkinson, Dana Densmore, Roxanne Dunbar, Germaine Greer, Rita Mae Brown, and Martha Shelley, among others, in groups like Boston's Cell 16, New York's Redstockings and The Feminists, or Washington, D.C.'s The Furies, wrote polemical articles exploring
4 the relationship between female sexuality and male domination."[4]
First published in 1968, Ann Koedt's essay "The Myth of the Vaginal Orgasm" was a massive catalyst for empowering women's sexual agency and questioning patriarchal power structures underlying conventional heterosexual relationships. In one of her most influential passages, Koedt writes, "We must discard 'normal' concepts of sex and create new guidelines which take into account mutual sexual enjoyment.... We must begin to demand that if certain sexual positions now defined as 'standard' are not mutually
5 conducive to orgasm, they no longer be defined as standard."[5]
Taking this feminist critique of heterosexual practice even further, Ti Grace Atkinson authored a pamphlet distributed by her political collective The Feminists in 1968 entitled "The Institution of Sexual Intercourse" in which she infamously decried heterosexual sex as "anti-feminist" and an "institution of patriarchal control."

3 Ibid., 115.

4 Jane Gerhard, "Revisiting 'The Myth of the Vaginal Orgasm': The Female Orgasm in American Sexual Thought and Second Wave Feminism," *Feminist Studies* Vol. 26, No. 2, Women and Health (Summer, 2000): 449.

5 Anne Koedt, "The Myth of the Vaginal Orgasm," in *Notes from the Second Year* (New York: New York Radical Feminists, 1970), p. 38.

Ever the contrarian, maverick British feminist Germaine Greer pushed back on some of these denunciations of the vagina in favour of clitoral-centric sexuality. In *The Female Eunuch* (1970), Greer advocated for a more holistic, sensuous, and individual sexuality. She cautions, "The banishment of the fantasy of the vaginal orgasm is ultimately a service, but the substantiation of the clitoral spasm for genuine gratification may turn out to be a disaster for sexuality… If we localize female response in the clitoris we impose upon women the same limitation of sex which has stunted the male's response."[6] Against this dissonant chorus of feminist voices, both Tompkins and Semmel produced a timely iconography that was inevitably read through the politics of female pleasure and sexual intercourse.

6 Germaine Greer, *The Female Eunuch*, (New York: McGraw-Hill Co., Inc. 1971; New York: Farrar, Straus and Giroux, 2001), p.48-49. Citation refers to Farrar, Straus and Giroux edition.

Political correctness and political intention were at the heart of the bifurcation of Semmel's and Tompkins' career paths. Semmel insisted on her interest in eroticism as being in alignment with the new feminist zeitgeist. At every possible turn, Semmel insisted on her paintings as depicting "the female perspective" and in her refusal of found imagery, unlike Tompkins' deployment of pornographic sources, she claimed a kind of ethical insurance policy that her painting did not involve any form of sexual exploitation or sex work. She even went so far as to carefully underline that the models she first drew, and later photographed, were never paid – she explains that she and a group of other women artists had met a male exhibitionist who volunteered to pose, and sometimes copulate, with his female partners for their artistic study. To further underscore the ethical and political intent of her work, Semmel was careful to emphasize her feminist credentials, her work as an activist, her membership in a women-centric artistic community, as well as her role as author and editor of a new art history entitled *A New Eros: Sexual Imagery in Women's Art*. Begun contemporaneously to her *Erotic Series*, Semmel compiled an archive of women's art and a collection of critical essays that were to be published by Hacker Art Books who formally contracted the publication in 1973. The book was to include contributions by some of the leading figures of the New York art world of the 1970s. Critic April Kingsley authored a visual survey of women's contemporary erotic art, Lucy Lippard, a key protagonist in New York's feminist ferment, wrote an essay on erotic abstraction, and anthropologist Elizabeth Weatherford contributed a chronicle of female sexuality and erotic imagery in ancient and non-Western societies. Judging from the unpublished manuscripts and slides that are today conserved in the Smithsonian Institute's Archives of American Art, Semmel's editorial project was extremely ambitious and had promised to be richly illustrated with a diverse range of artists' work including

Colette, Agnes Denes, Mary Beth Edelson, Nancy Grossman, Marisol, Alice Neel, Niki de Saint Phalle, Sylvia Sleigh, as well as fellow Fight Censorship members Judith Bernstein, Louise Bourgeois, Martha Edelheit, Eunice Golden, Juanita McNeely, Ann Sharp, and Hannah Wilke.

Drawing in part from the new consensus formed around the FC Group, Semmel's introductory essay argues for a broad new category of art and a specific agency for women artists rooted in the domain of the erotic. She writes, "From vaginal iconography to the male nude, from phallic symbols to androgynous biomorphic shapes, from figurines fucking to menstruating mothers, the prolonged probe of women's art touches on the raw nerves of a system whose most basic structure is being questioned... The sexual theme touches on the most universal and personal kind of human experience, one in which the female has always been deeply involved but seldom permitted to comment upon. Suddenly, in all the arts, women are today dealing with the heretofore forbidden. We finally realize that the need to express ourselves as we really are, in all of our aspects, is a vital necessity if we are to break the invisible chains which have immobilized us for centuries. It is time to see ourselves through our own eyes!"[7]

7 Joan Semmel, *A New Eros: Sexual Imagery in Women's Art.* Unpublished manuscript, 1973. Joan Semmel fonds, Archives of American Art Smithsonian Institution, Joan Semmel papers, 1949-2013, Box 3.

While liberationist in tone, Semmel's call to arms for this sexualist art as a "mainstream movement", along with the six commissioned essays and the extensive documentation she painstakingly compiled, would never see the bookstore or the library shelf. While Semmel continued to work on the book through 1976, Hacker sent her a letter explaining that "feminism was over" and that the book no longer would find an audience. While she continued to search for a publisher through the 1980s, the manuscript languished in Semmel's studio and eventually was acquired by the Smithsonian's Archives of American Art. Despite this disappointing turn of events, her activities as a political activist and vocal theorist of women's erotic art has long helped to bolster her position in the canon of feminist art.

Betty Tompkins' *Fuck Paintings* were very deliberately omitted from the manuscript of Semmel's *A New Eros*, despite the obvious overlap in subject matter. While Semmel was clearly aware of Tompkins' practice when she was assembling her book, Tompkins didn't make the cut because her work was seen as crossing a red line: Semmel objected to Tompkins' appropriation of mainstream pornography. Tompkins' deliberate exclusion also extended to the feminist artistic and political groups that Semmel participated in and whose membership played a large role in the professional opportunities in the New York art scene of the 1970s.

While Tompkins was included in a group exhibition at Lo Giudice Gallery in 1973 that focused on the then new trend of photorealism in painting, she attributed her preclusion from feminist art circles in SoHo to her polemical subject matter and source material. With over fifty years of hindsight, Tompkins reconciles her exclusion with a positive spin. "Being excluded from the feminist art movement gave me a lot of freedom. I read the books and articles, but I was free to pick and choose. I wasn't subject to any social pressure. I am better off for it. Artists like Joan Semmel had tied their work to theory. I had grown up around leftist politics, and grew up with theory. I saw the arguments and the divisions. It didn't help anyone."[8] In addition to her apolitical stance and position as an outlier, Tompkins further suffered the dehabilitating consequences of censorship with her *Fuck Paintings*.

8 Betty Tompkins in discussion with the author, 14 February 2018.

It wasn't until the late 1970s that pornography became an official flashpoint within the feminist movement when it effectively cleaved women into warring camps for and against. And while they were never in direct, open conflict, the schism that was perceived in the meaning of the explicit eroticism of Joan Semmel's and Betty Tompkins' oeuvres anticipated so many of the ferocious tensions that surround the politics of sexuality, free speech and the debates around sex work. An anti-pornography feminist position was articulated in late 1970s America by feminist activists Andrea Dworkin and lawyer Catherine McKinnon. Together, they co-authored "civil rights ordinances that deemed pornography as legally actionable sex discrimination," based on the assertion that "graphically sexually explicit materials subordinate women through pictures or words."[9] The protest group Women Against Pornography also emerged in 1979 in parallel to Dworkin and McKinnon's discursive work and legal actions in this realm to organize numerous demonstrations and direct actions in New York. Their most visible protest march was held in Times Square in October 1979, drawing over five thousand participants and garnering widespread press coverage. Bold faced feminist veterans such as Bella Abzug, Susan Brownmiller, Gloria Steinem, and Robin Morgan participated in these actions on the pretext that there is a direct causal relationship between pornography and rape, sexual harassment and bigotry against women. The foundation of WAP and its anti-pornography advocacy further polarized feminist debate into a single issue around porn that dominated the discourse for decades. It could even be argued that the effects of the pornography rows as well as the influence of the Women Against Pornography movement over mainstream '80s and '90s feminism in America further forestalled the reception of Tompkins' work until the turn of the 21st century.

9 Drucilla Cornell, *Feminism and Pornography* (Oxford: Oxford University Press, 2000), p. 3

Semmel's careful distinctions about creating her own imagery and not partaking in a sexual economy exempted her from transgressing any ethical or moral boundaries. Semmel reiterated these boundaries in 2016, "I was not appropriating pornography. I was trying to make work that was about sex, that was different to pornography and that had the sense of how a woman feels about sex; what turns a woman on. I felt that most pornography was predicated on what turns a man on. I felt that was going to be the difference in my work, between pornography and what I call art. So that was a very important distinction for me. Everybody felt differently about it." Tompkins' lack of declared political affiliation and unrepentant, untheorized use of found pornographic imagery from her husband's collection set herself up for suspicion. Yet when juxtaposing their works side by side, the formal similarities are striking. Tompkins' *Fuck Painting #1* (1969) and Semmel's *Purple Passion* (1973) depict an identical scene: the act of heterosexual penetration with the man on the bottom and the woman on top. On each canvas, the woman's buxom behind dominates the composition and the viewer's eye is drawn to the man's erect penis and scrotum below her sensuous body. Both are painted without expressive brush marks, with Tompkins using her signature grisaille palette and Semmel deploying the non-naturalistic chromatic exuberance that has come to define this body of work. Tompkins' treatment of the image is more tightly cropped, focusing exclusively on the sex act whereas Semmel uses a wider shot that includes the man's hands, the woman's back and both of their legs. Despite these differences, the nature of the act depicted is identical. Is not Semmel's attempt to depict her female "desire" in this act of penetration almost identical to the desire depicted by the 1950s pornographer? In this instance, what besides expressionist use of colour differentiates pornography from a women's authorship of erotic imagery? Do cropping or chromatic decisions define the frontier between the pornographic and empowered, feminist-sanctioned eroticism? If politicizing context and intent is removed from the digestion of these paintings, it is difficult to make an ethical distinction between the coitus paintings by Semmel and Tompkins in this instance.

"I enjoy doing my research," is about as much as Betty will say about the subject of pornography itself. Without recourse to a political pronunciation, moral or personal narrative justification for her use of these charged found images, the pornographic in Tompkins' work becomes an unstable signifier. As such, the threat implied by the pornographic signifier has long overshadowed Tompkins' oeuvre—the political incorrectness of her source material is perhaps more powerful than the phallic imagery itself.

Betty Tompkins' work acts via seizure and claiming authorship as a symbolic phallus – defined in psychoanalytic terms, the phallus is a symbol of power. To paraphrase Jacques Lacan, the phallus is something men strive to have, and women try to be. Here, the phallus takes the form of pornography-as-readymade, traditionally the domain of male power and pleasure. Tompkins uses it for her own aesthetic purposes, transforming it into a powerful painted icon that transforms the found image via cropping, magnifying scale and removing colour. It is through Tompkins' double seizure of the phallus – both as a literal image of the erect penis and the signifier of mainstream pornography – that her art was perceived as a threat to even the most radical fringes of second-wave feminist artists.

Belated Career

As a result of her systemic exclusion as well as the obvert censorship, Tompkins literally rolled up her monumental *Fuck Paintings* at the close of the 1970s and put them in storage in her loft. She made a living teaching for the next three decades. (A surreal side note: the boundary-pushing comedienne Joan Rivers was a private oil painting student of Tompkins in the late 1990s.) Teaching did not stop her from making work: she created a series of paintings on paper based on foundational legal texts such as the Constitution and the Bill of Rights – the word "LAW" appears in the backdrop, repeated in all caps, like a defiant protest chant. Reminiscent of fragmented illuminated manuscripts, these pieces attest to Tompkins' struggle against censure while redressing her earliest childhood memories.

Tompkins was born in Washington D.C. in 1945 and raised in Philadelphia. Her father was the head of the Philadelphia chapter of the left-wing Progressive Party – a controversial association in an age of Cold War paranoia. "My first complete sentence was, 'Do you have a search warrant?'" Tompkins scoffs, "when I was a toddler with a five-word vocabulary!" The FBI regularly followed her and her sister to school, "because the government was very anti-liberal, anti-socialist and anti-communist." It is hard not to see these formative childhood experiences as a source of Tompkins' fortitude in asserting her rights as a citizen, an artist and a woman. "It was a really fascinating way to be raised and it prepared me for what my adulthood would become," she says." I wasn't so interested in belonging to systems and groups."

Only at the turn of the 21st century was Tompkins given an opportunity to show in New York – and this time it was on her own terms. In 2002, a New York City public school teacher-turned-gallerist called Mitchell Algus finally had the guts to exhibit her full cycle of *Fuck Paintings*. "Jerry Saltz came into the gallery around 2000, or early 2001 and handed me a sheet of slides that Betty had sent to him," Algus recalls, "I immediately called her." Ever the art world tastemaker, Saltz was at that time serving as the art critic at the *Village Voice*. "I used to get a lot of unsolicited slides from artists. I looked at them all. Then came Betty Tompkins' slides. They sizzled. Still," gushes Saltz. "I called Betty; she was the real deal, obviously. I remember thinking, 'This is how free art is! Women are finally getting to tell their stories.'" With Saltz's endorsement and Algus' commitment to unearthing artists who have been hidden in plain sight, the stage was set. As Algus recalls, "The fact that they were rolled up appealed to me." When asked if he was nervous about debuting the *Fuck Paintings*, Algus asserts, "They were good paintings and that was their defense. If that was not the case, it would have fallen flat."

With critical momentum from Saltz and support from esteemed fellow artists (Robert Gober and Donald Moffat were among the first to buy a painting from this 2002 show), critics finally paid attention and the censors were kept (albeit temporarily) at bay. The *New York Times* art critic Holland Cotter shouted out Tompkins' belated debut as "formidable" in an article entitled "Two Nods to Feminism, Long Snubbed by Curators." Artist Marilyn Minter still remembers Tompkins' breakthrough show. "When I first saw her hardcore images at Mitchell Algus I couldn't believe my eyes," Minter raves, "Honestly, my first thought was 'Damn, I thought I was the first,' but I also thought about how much braver she was than me and how much shame must have been thrown at her back in the '70s. Being officially censored by the government was truly scary stuff." Speaking of the history of severe backlash that she shares with Tompkins, Minter continues, "Most art people were so frightened about any women owning sexual agency. It was such a threat to the status quo back then and still today...unfortunately." Saltz also acknowledges this ongoing struggle, "the world still fears women picturing dicks and blow-jobs." Nevertheless, Tompkins' 2002 outing received the first of many critical appraisals that would help reinsert Tompkins into art history and a larger feminist conversation.

By that time, feminist discourse had become less polarized and more diverse. The anti-pornography wing of American feminism had lost its stranglehold, allowing for a range of positions on sexual speech into the mainstream and giving credence to more sex-positive feminisms. Despite the high emotional and financial toll, Betty Tompkins' work prevailed as a commentary on sexual free speech and revindication of sex work.

Tompkins did not waste any time given this second chance to build her artistic profile. After her debut show with Algus, she made a slow but steady climb out of obscurity. As the news spread about her extraordinary story and revisionist art histories began to incorporate Tompkins' work into the narrative of 20th century art, invitations to show in galleries, museums and biennales gradually started to arrive in Tompkins' inbox. *Fuck Painting #1* was acquired by Paris' Centre Pompidou – a glorious outcome for a painting that spent thirty years rolled up under the artist's pool table. With this new approbation, Tompkins not only returned to making *Fuck Paintings*; she jubilantly expanded the range of her work, no longer limited to her original trove of miniature porn photos. With the savvy of a millennial, she mined the internet for material and advocated for her work on social media. Like a warrior who has awoken from a forced hibernation, Tompkins engaged with new fronts on the battlefield of free speech and gender equity. Her very presence on Instagram has been one of these frontlines.

Since she joined the platform in 2015, Tompkins' posts of her paintings have been regularly taken down – reported as "inappropriate." In the spring of 2019, her account was deleted. After protesting with the help of other artists, she got it reinstated, and was invited by Instagram to participate in a closed-door roundtable with other artists and cultural figures about censorship.

"As it turned out, I couldn't be there", she recalls. "So I asked if it would be okay to write something that could be then read at the panel so it's in the record." Tompkins spent weeks wracking her brain trying to articulate the difference between the kind of government censure she received in the 1970s and this corporate episode of policing. Instagram, after all, is not a public utility or a public space, therefore not subject to the rule of law or rights guaranteed by the Constitution.

"I said to myself, you actually never did read their community guidelines. So I read them and I was simultaneously so fucking angry and laughing so hard that I threw out all of my ideas and sat down and wrote a short statement." When it comes to nudity, Tompkins learned that Instagram rules allow for certain images such as nursing babies or mastectomy scars. "And I quote, 'Photos of nudity in painting and sculpture is okay too.' After reading that, I wrote a statement for their panel that simply said, 'These are your community guidelines, follow them, do better.' That was my whole statement."

And while Tompkins is still subjected to deleted posts and occasional account shut-downs (explained away as "mistakes" by Instagram, due to high user volume), she has never shied away from holding the platform to their terms of use or publicly calling out their hypocrisies. Tompkins will not be silenced – and like in the 1970s, she has immortalized images of posts deleted by Instagram as the basis of a new series of *Censored* paintings.

The same timely quest for justice drives Tompkins' most recent body of work. Under the umbrella title *Apologia*, Tompkins draws upon the transcripts of public *mea culpas* by some of the most egregious sexual abusers who have been toppled by the #MeToo movement. She has hand painted these texts onto reproductions of famous paintings torn out of art history books – the words shrouding the central female figures. Using her signature hue of Bazooka pink paint, Tompkins meticulously transcribes the language used to cover up or redeem bad behaviour. These pathetic "lamentations" are excerpted from press statements by notorious offenders such as Harvey Weinstein, Les Moonves, Mario Batali, Matt Lauer, Knight Landesman, Louis CK, and Charlie Rose among many others. In addition to highlighting the falsehoods and rhetorical backpedaling of these alleged predators, Tompkins also transforms reproductions of familiar works by artists such as Caravaggio, Ingres and Degas by covering the female figures with the toxic language. Or as Tompkins explains, the overlaying of the women in these art historical images with these *Apologia* scripts is like "putting her in a shroud: you're obliterating her, hiding her with words."

In other pieces, Tompkins overpaints the male figures in works by historical women artists – such as Artemisia Gentileschi's biblical scene *Jael and Sisera* (1620). Obscuring the supine figure of the general Sisera, who is about to be murdered by Jael, Tompkins superimposes the words of artist Chuck Close accused of sexual misconduct by numerous young women: "It's lies. I haven't slept in weeks. I've been such a supporter of women and women artists. I've done nothing wrong and I'm being crucified."

Tompkins' textual interventions confront the distortions of history while holding up a mirror to our present-day reckoning with systemic abuses of power: "One day I thought, 'Art History!' What I saw was hundreds and hundreds and hundreds of years of misogyny in the art world coming right up to my face and giving itself to me as a present."

It's tempting to interpret the *Apologia* series as an implicit rebuke of a college professor who once told her, "The only way you're making it in New York, honey, is on your back." And although decades separate the pieces that scared off gallerists in the 1970s and her most recent word paintings, they are united by Tompkins' will to transform or reclaim forces that seek to silence her. Tompkins' fearless example has paved the way for a whole new generation of artists who continue the battle over sexual free speech, expanding beyond the feminist debates of the '70s to explore and represent queer and non-heteronormative erotic imaginaries. She may have started out as an accidental dissident, but Tompkins has grown to harness her monumentally defiant spirit. The moral of this art historical tale? Don't fuck with Betty Tompkins.

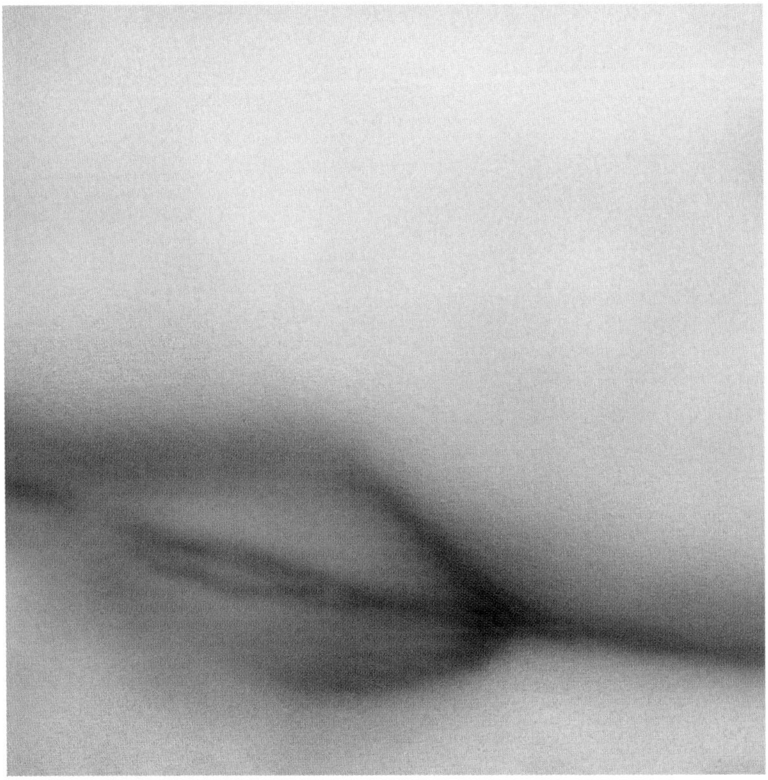

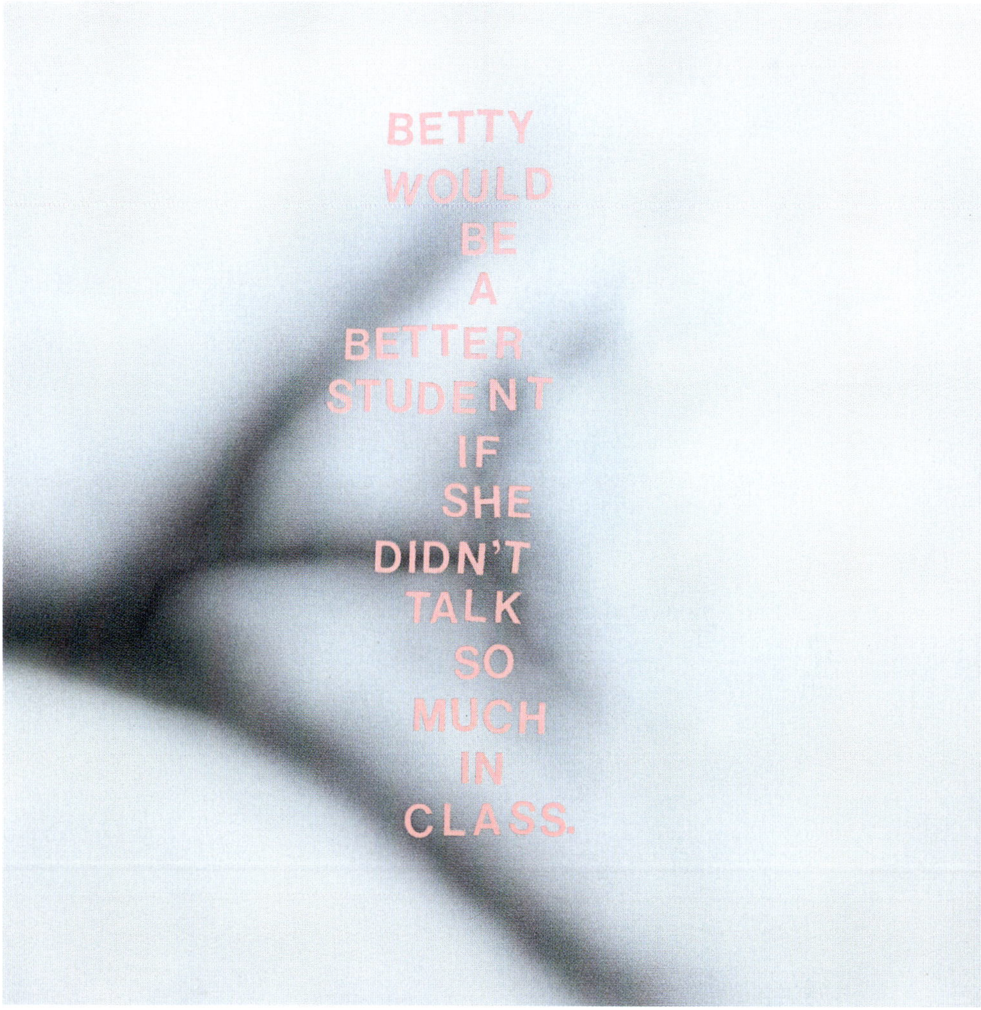
BETTY
WOULD
BE
A
BETTER
STUDENT
IF
SHE
DIDN'T
TALK
SO
MUCH
IN
CLASS.

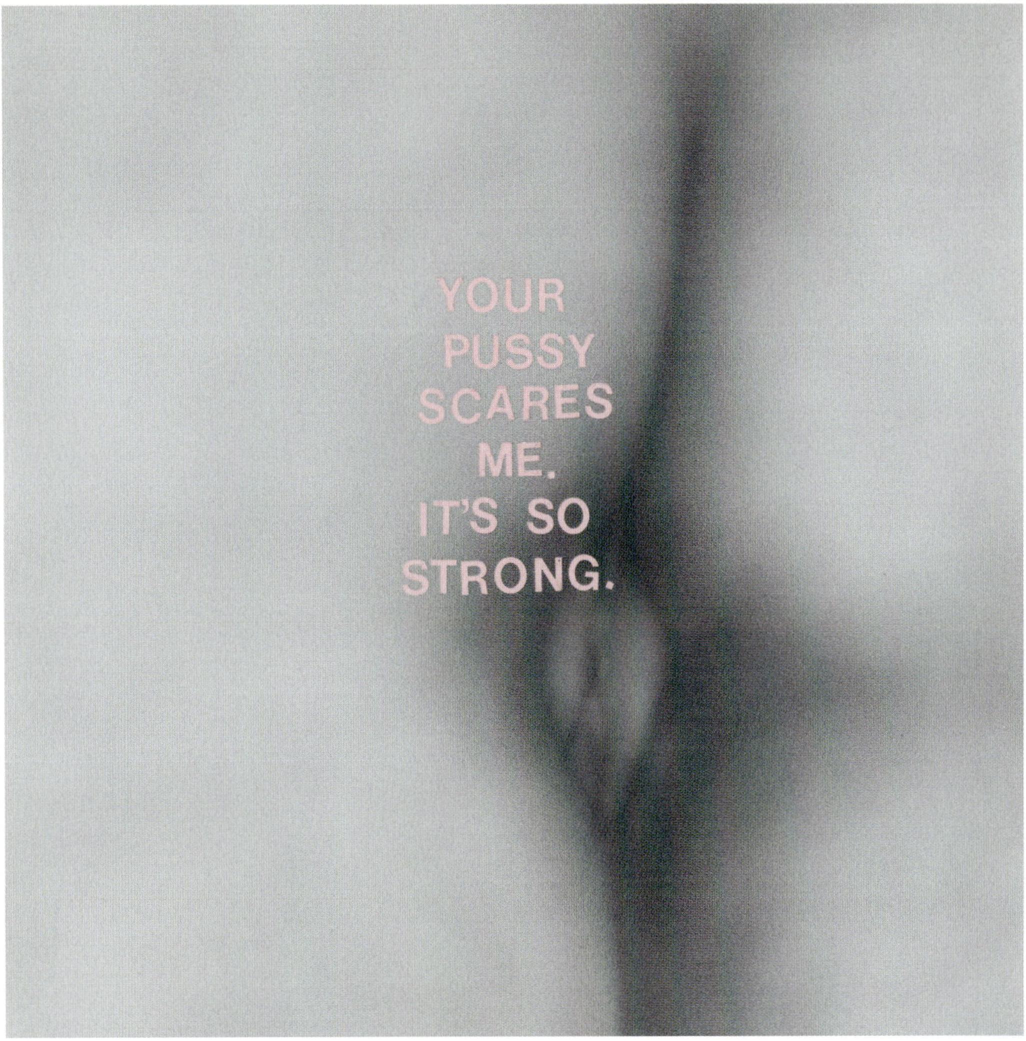
YOUR
PUSSY
SCARES
ME.
IT'S SO
STRONG.

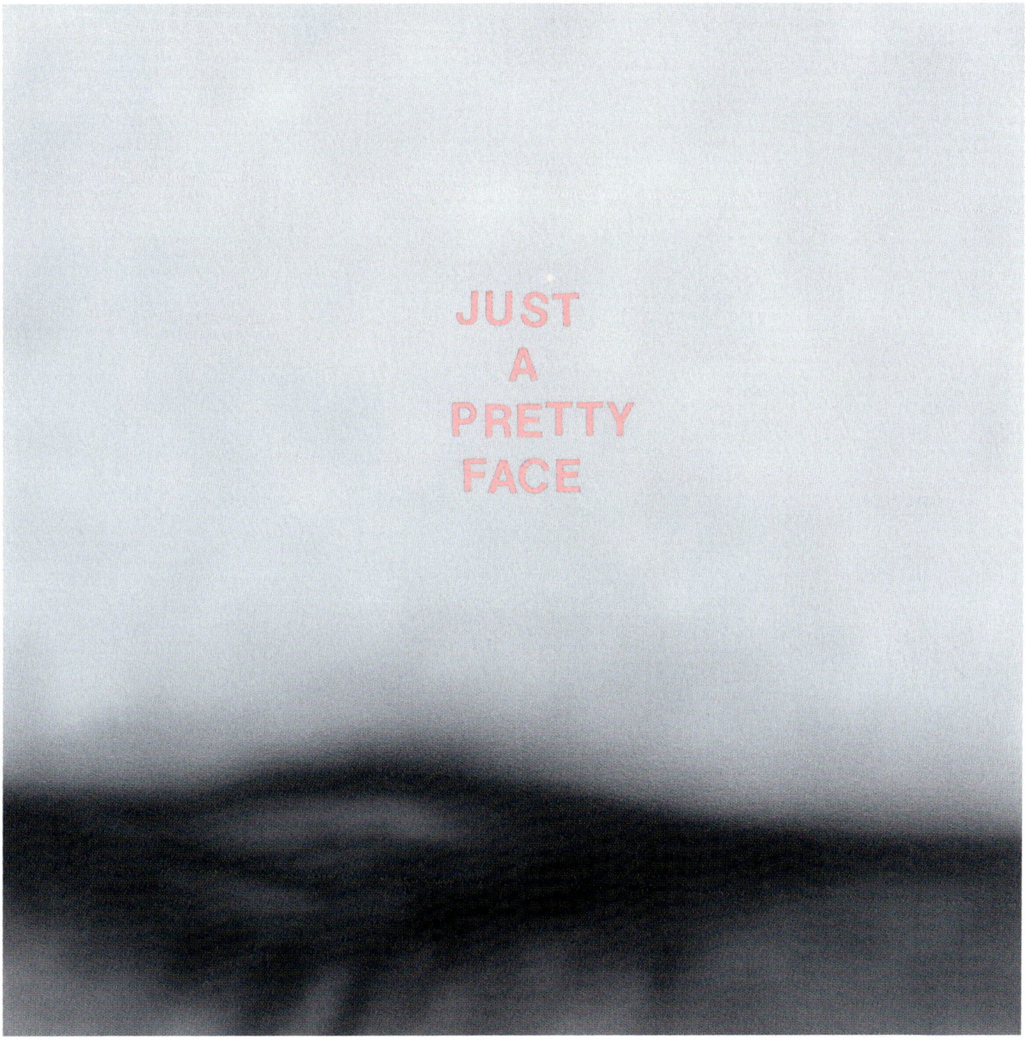
JUST
A
PRETTY
FACE

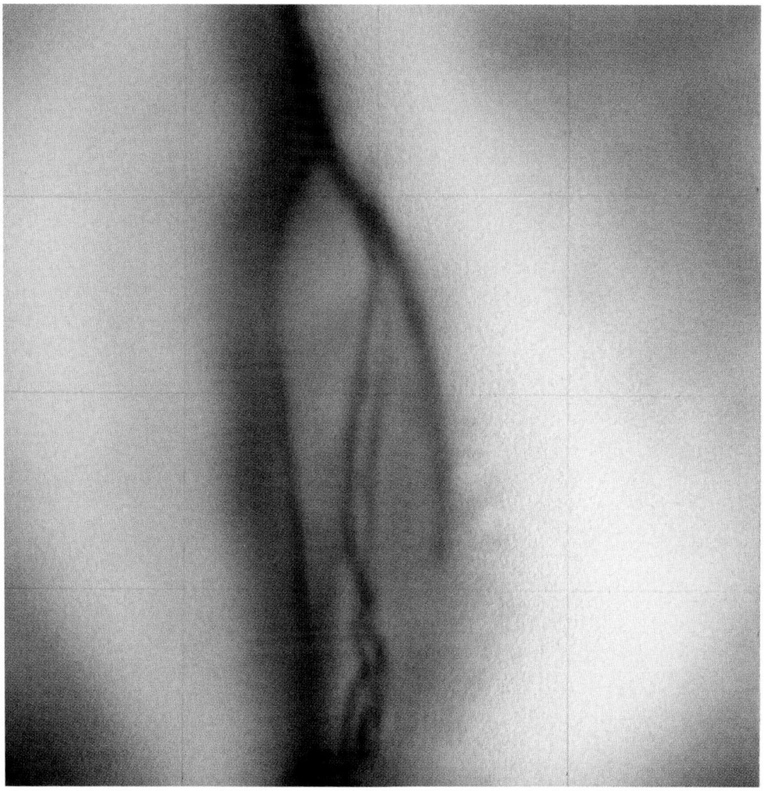

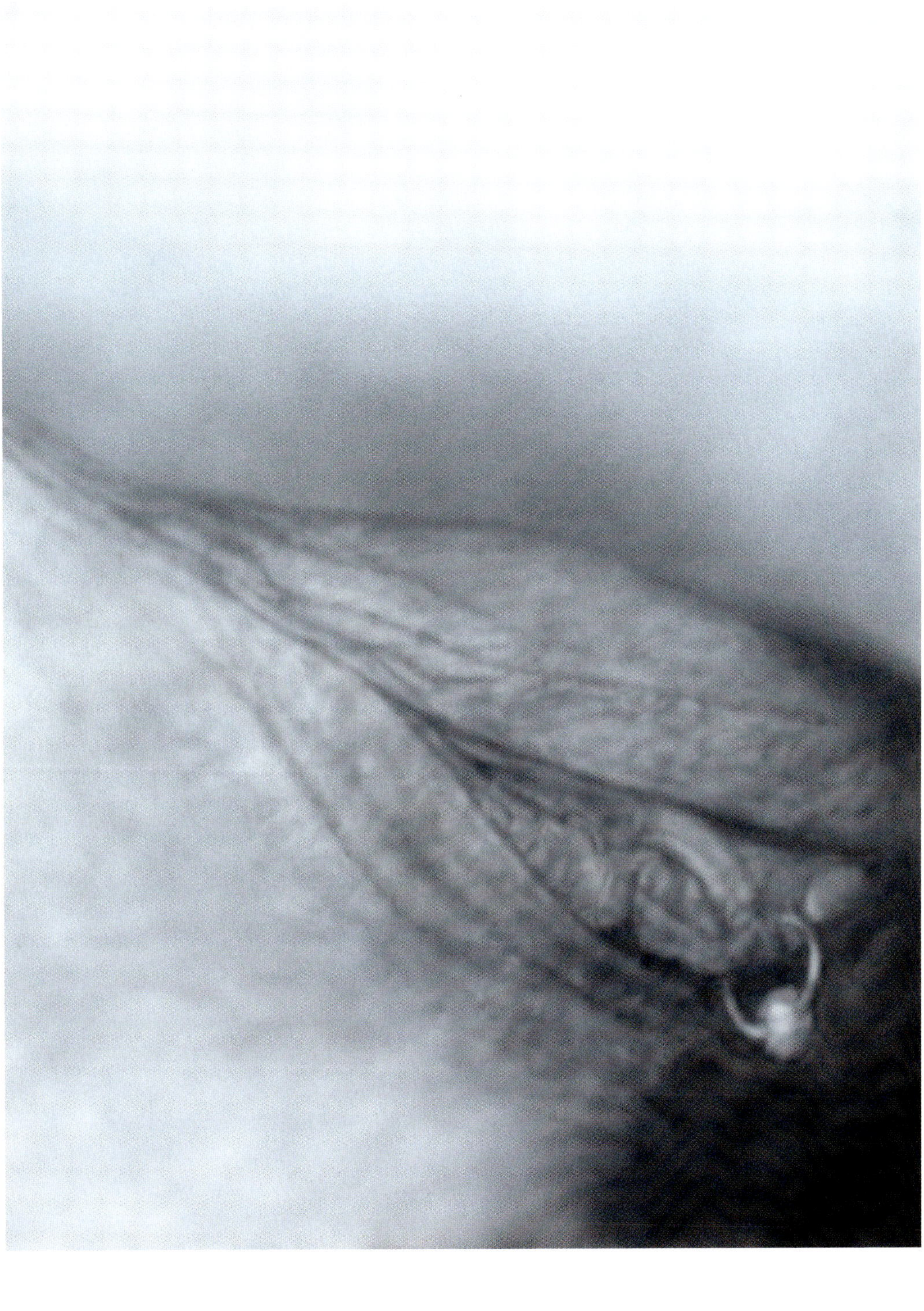

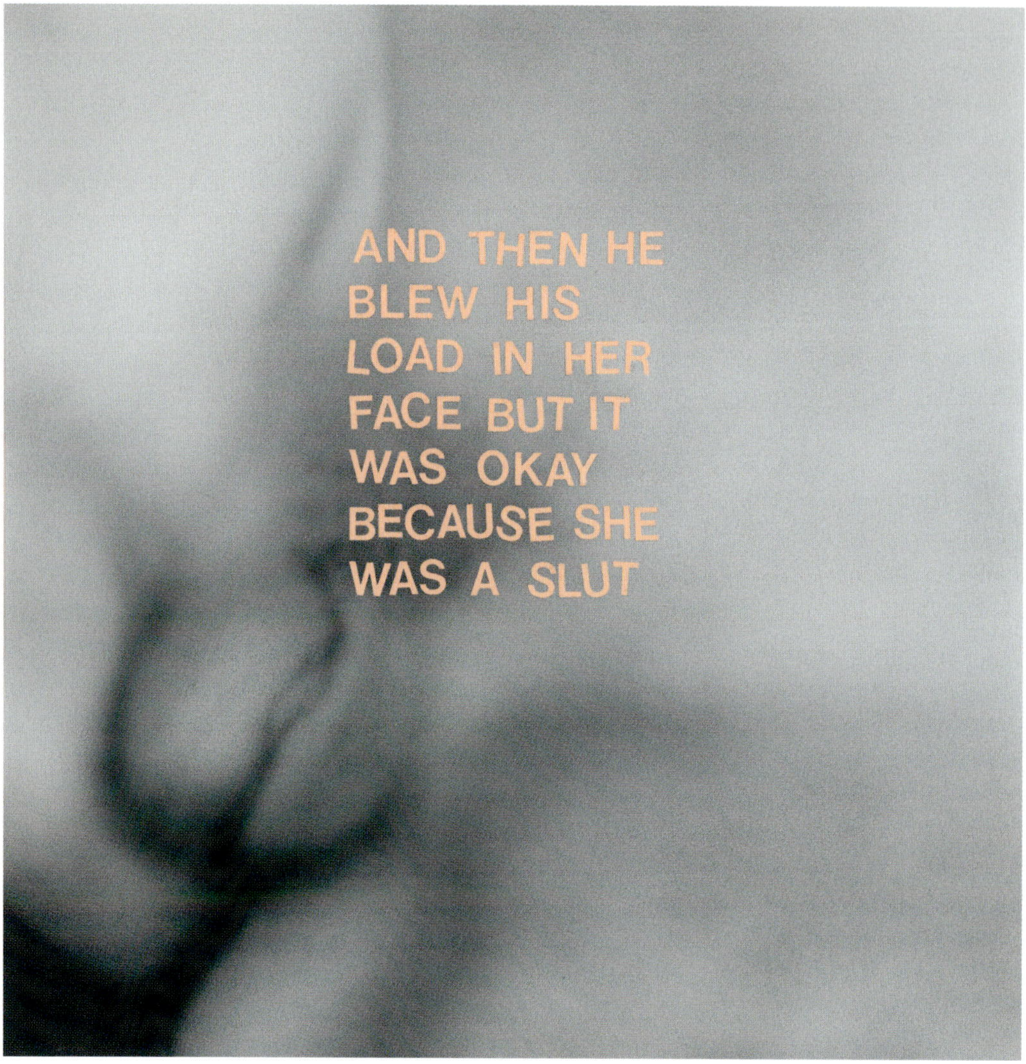
AND THEN HE
BLEW HIS
LOAD IN HER
FACE BUT IT
WAS OKAY
BECAUSE SHE
WAS A SLUT

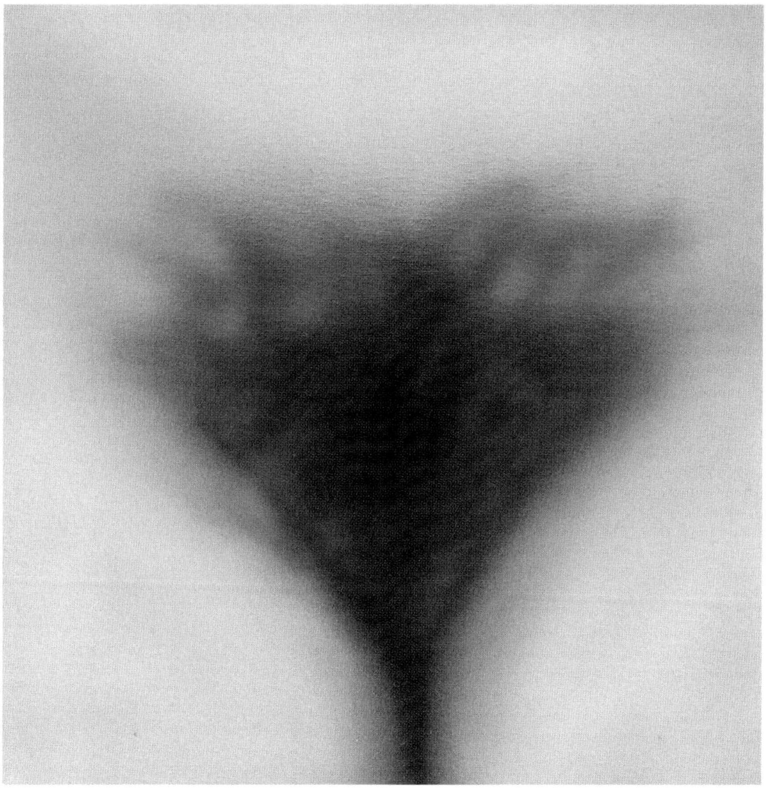

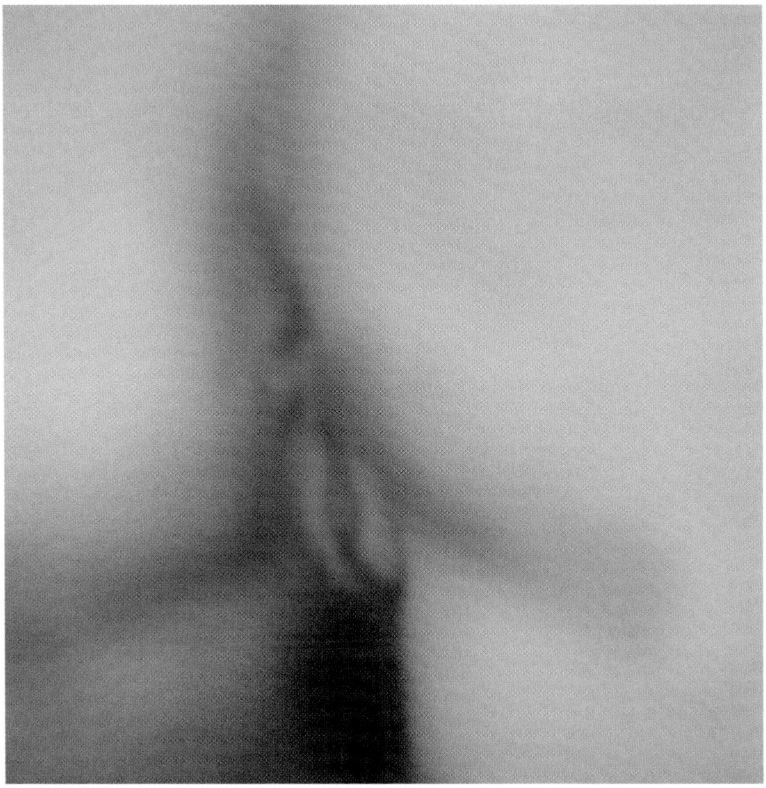

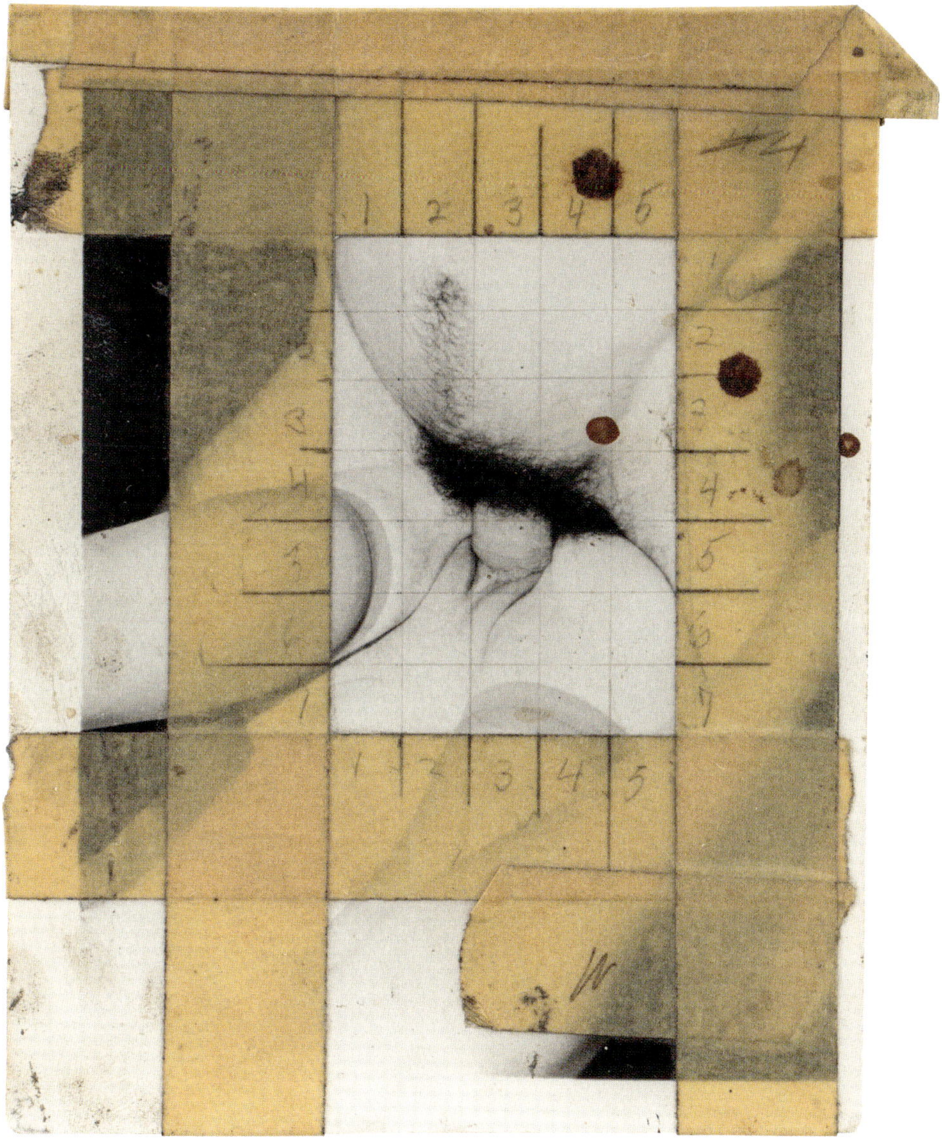

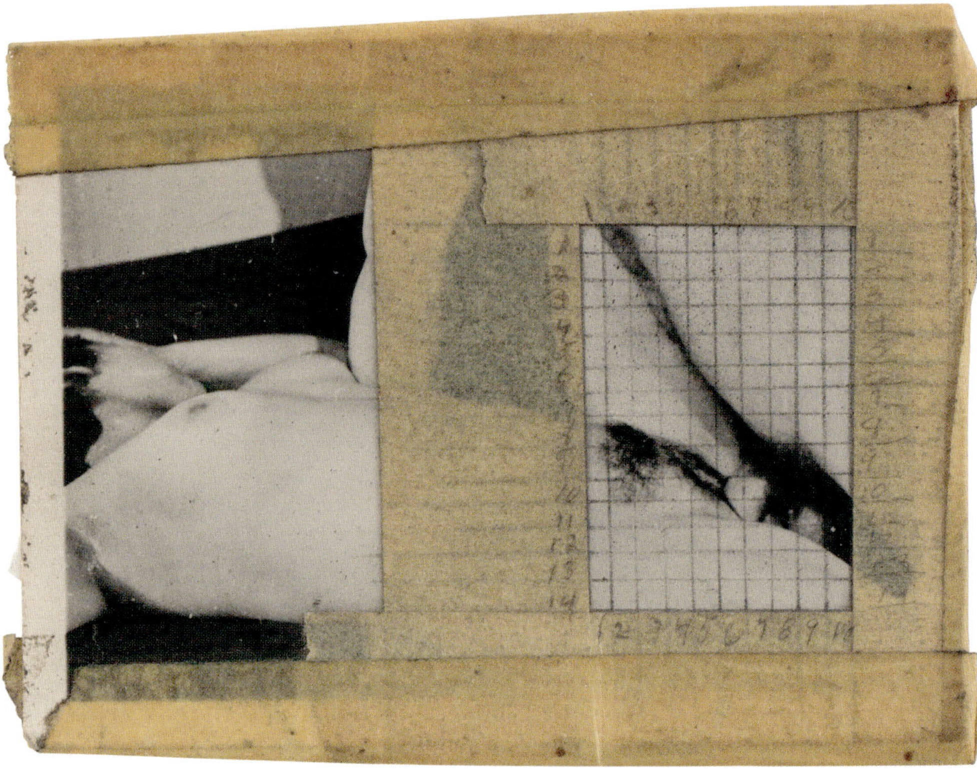

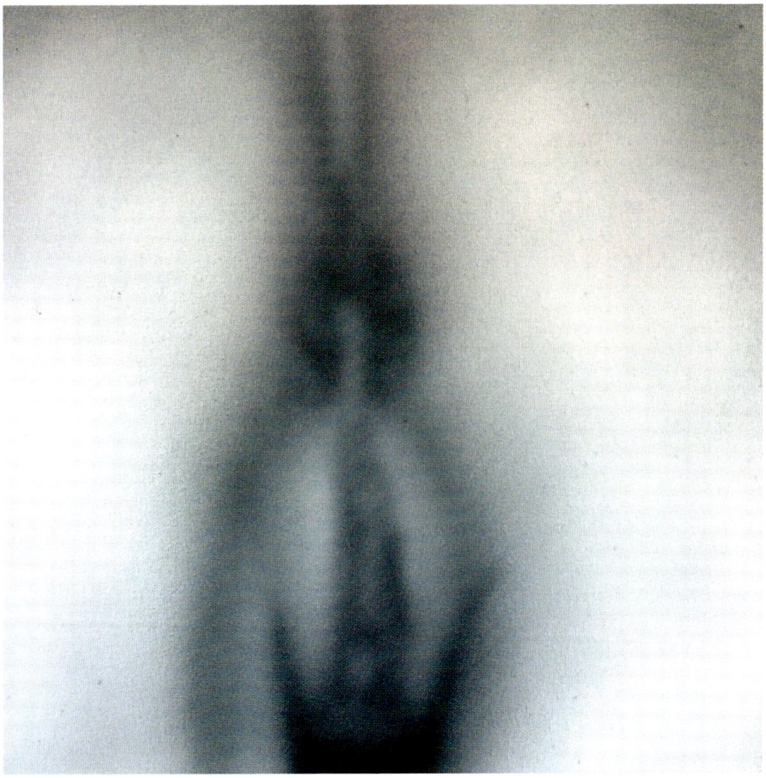

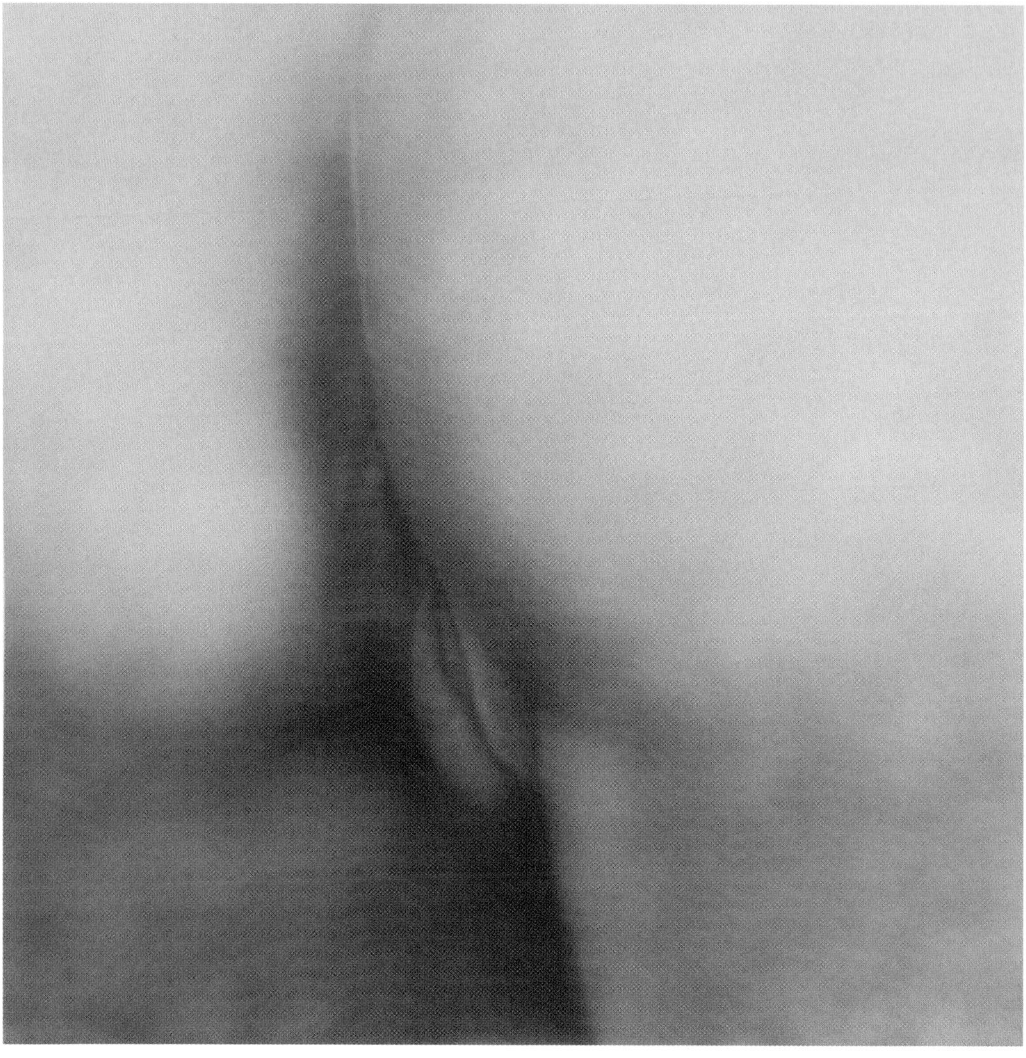

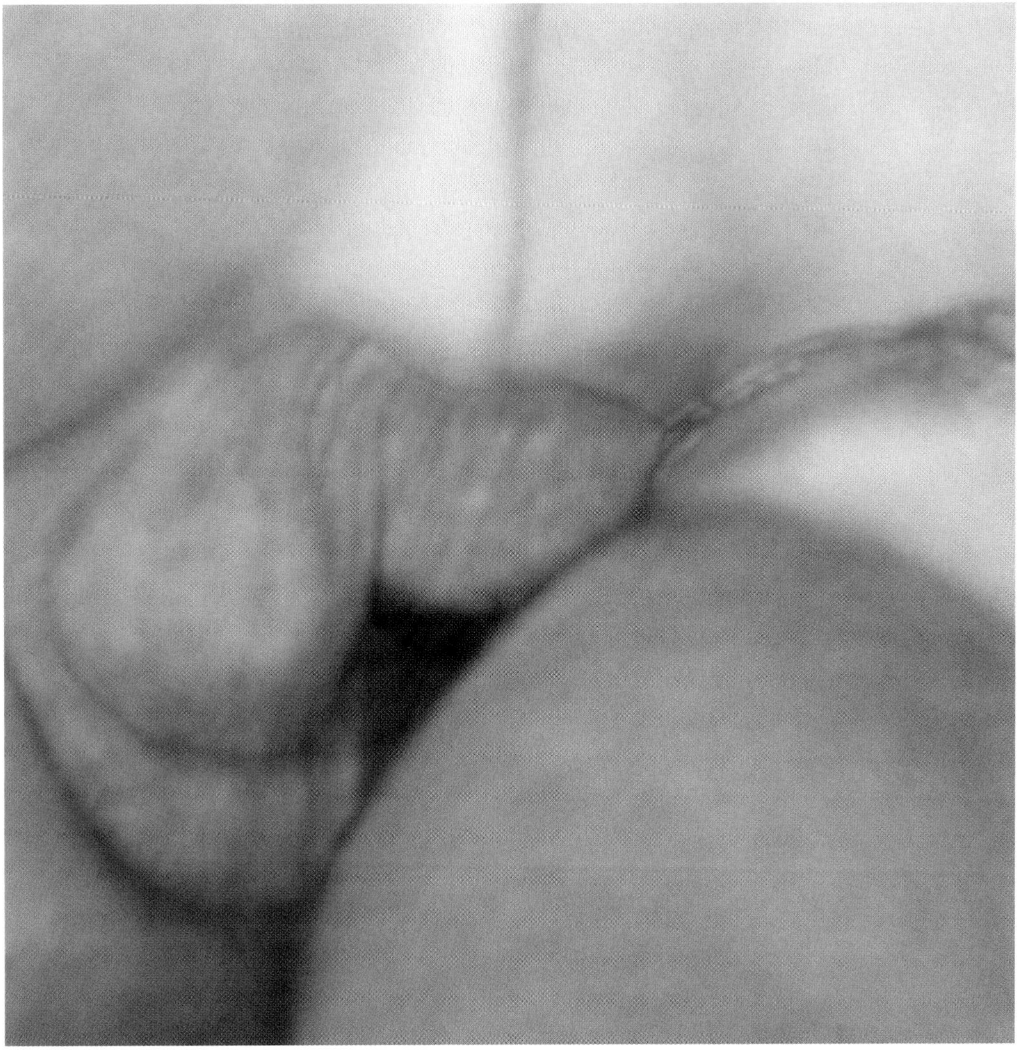

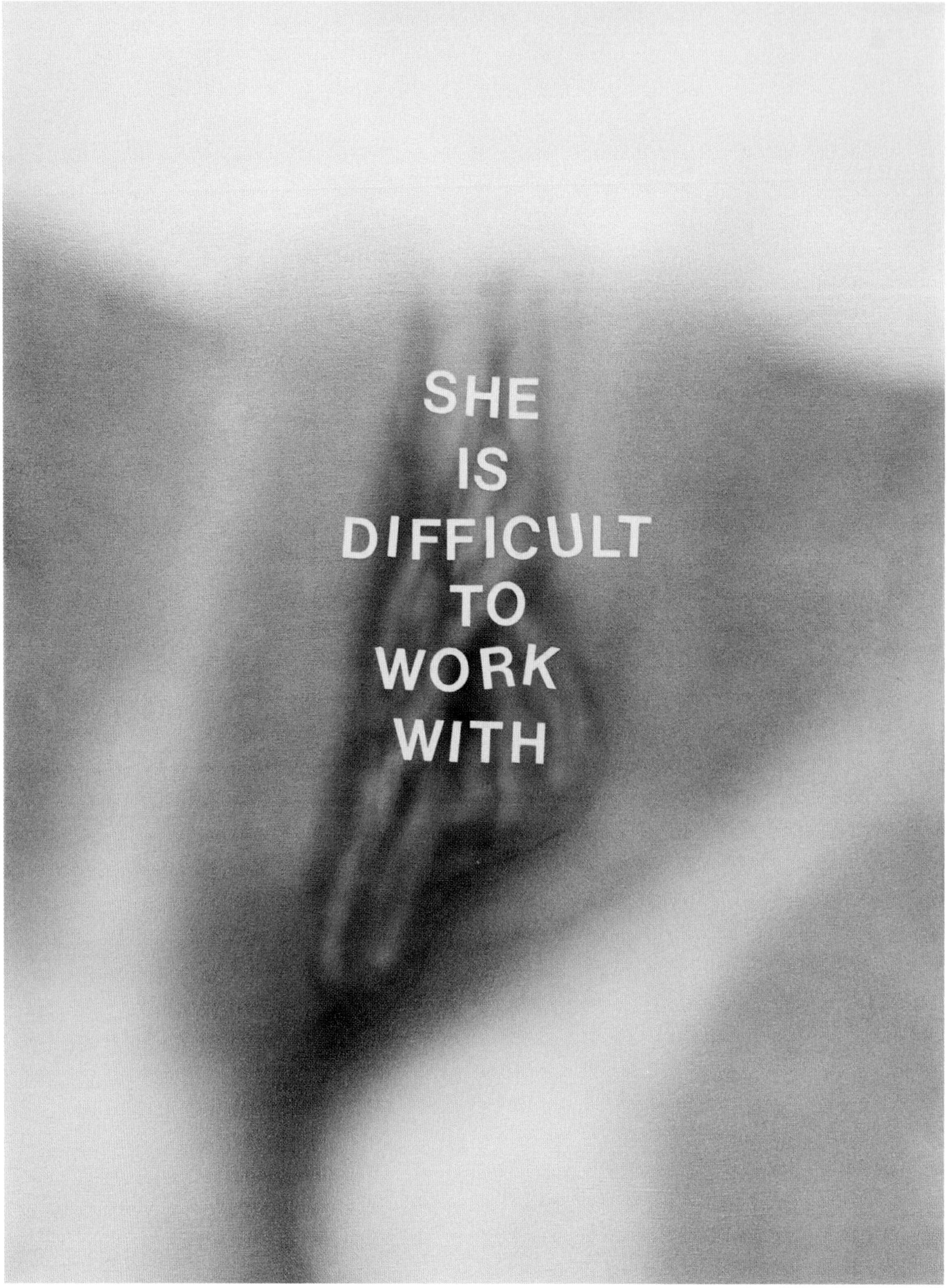
SHE
IS
DIFFICULT
TO
WORK
WITH

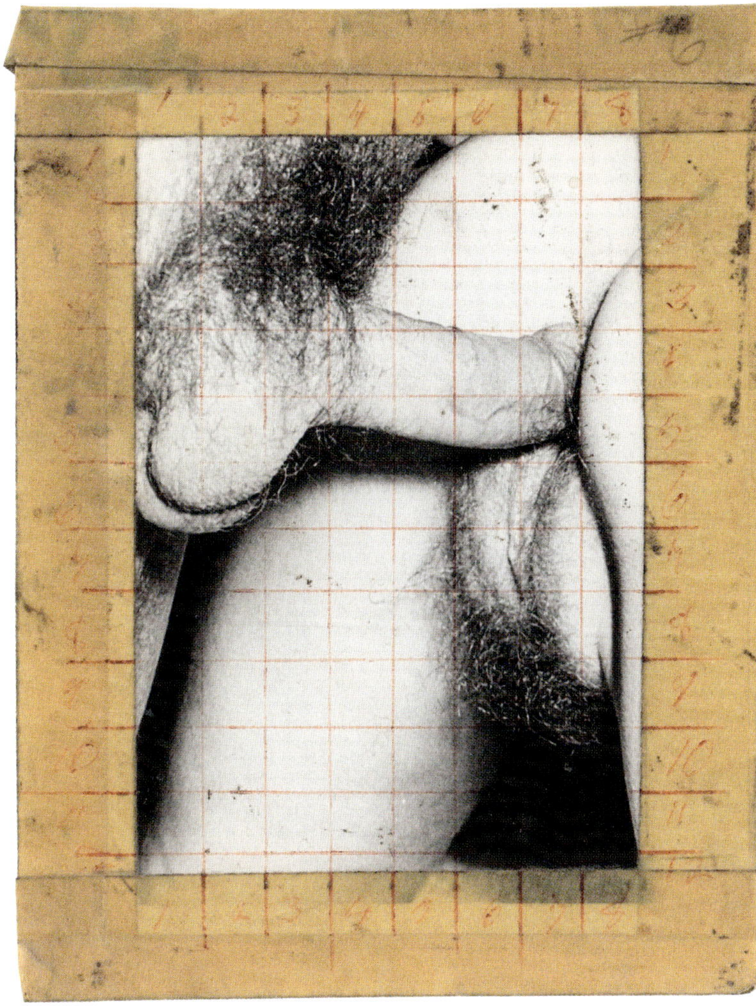

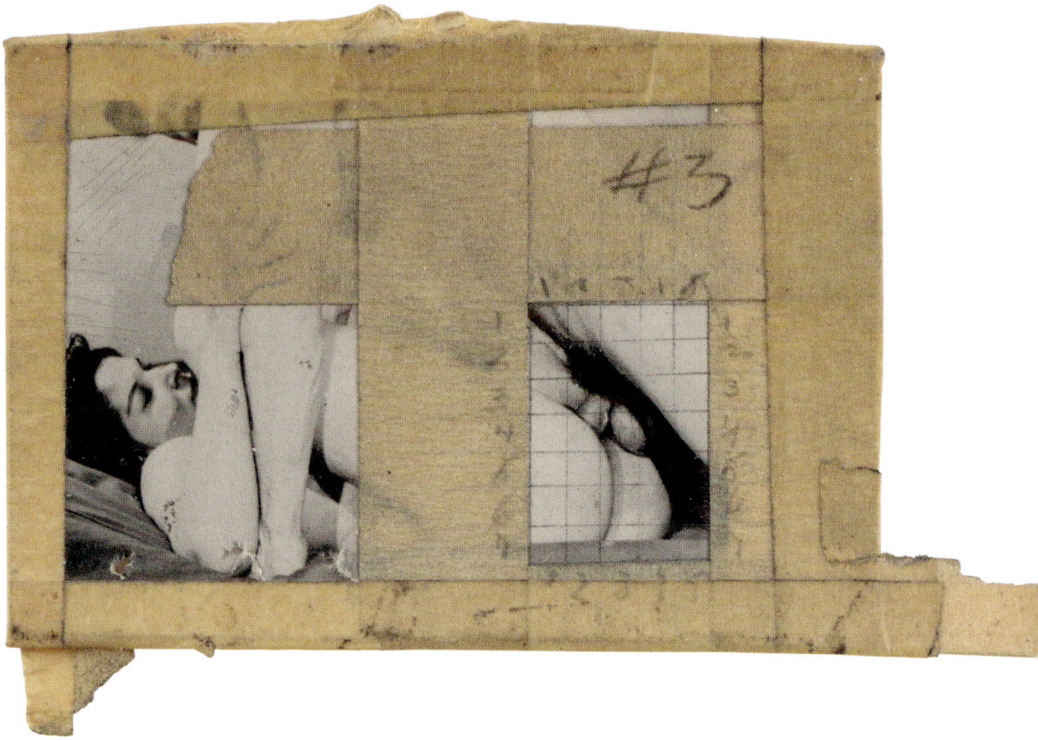
43

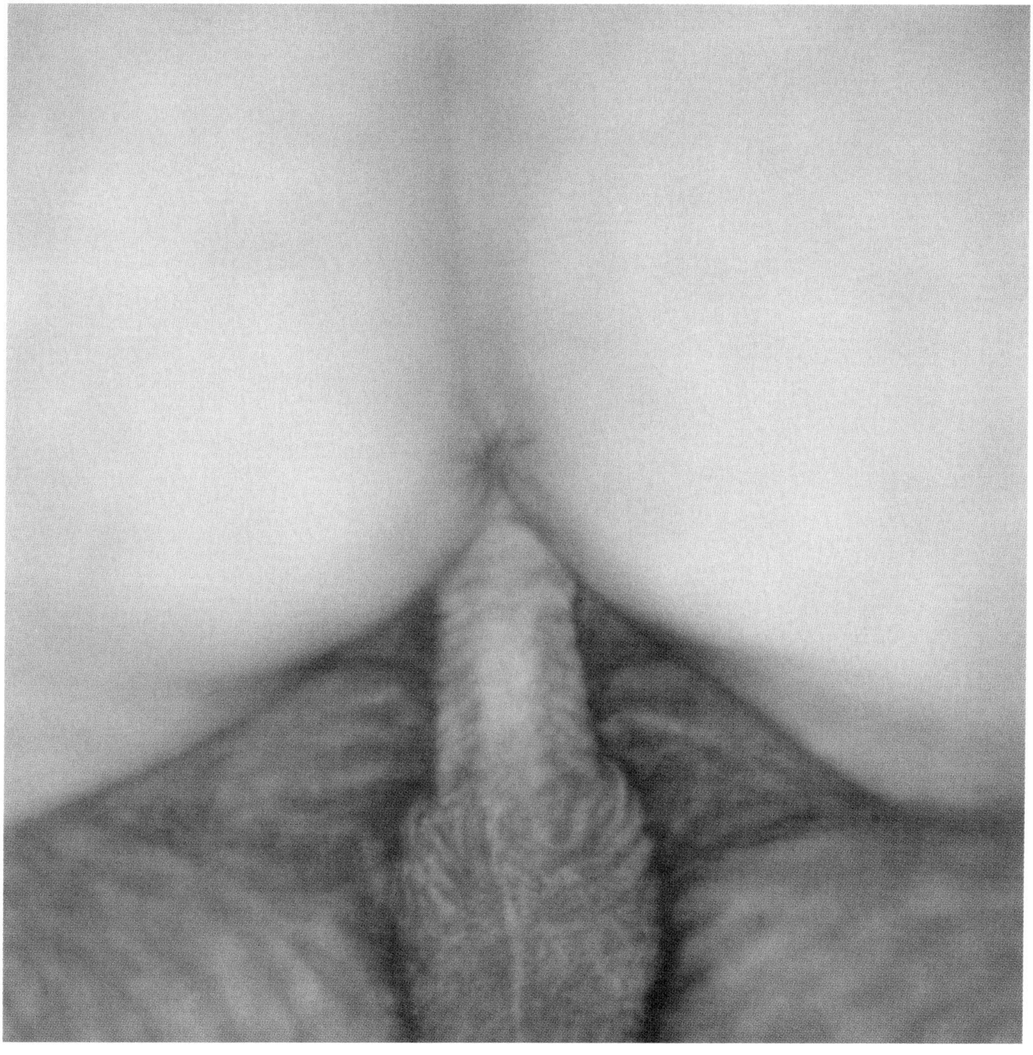

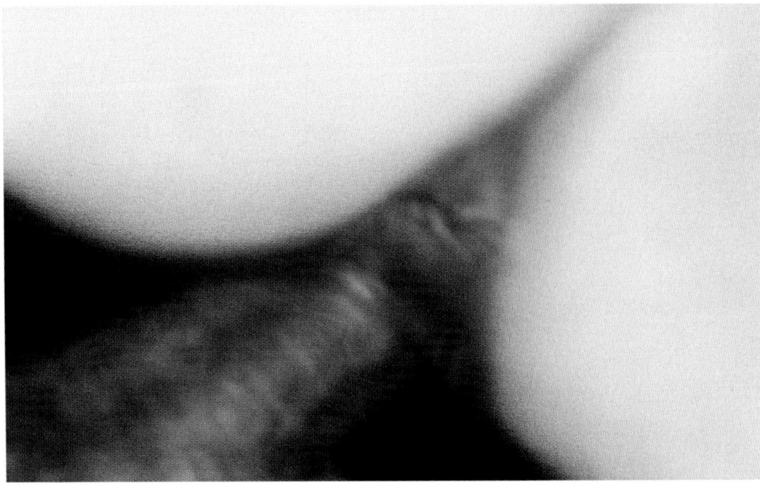

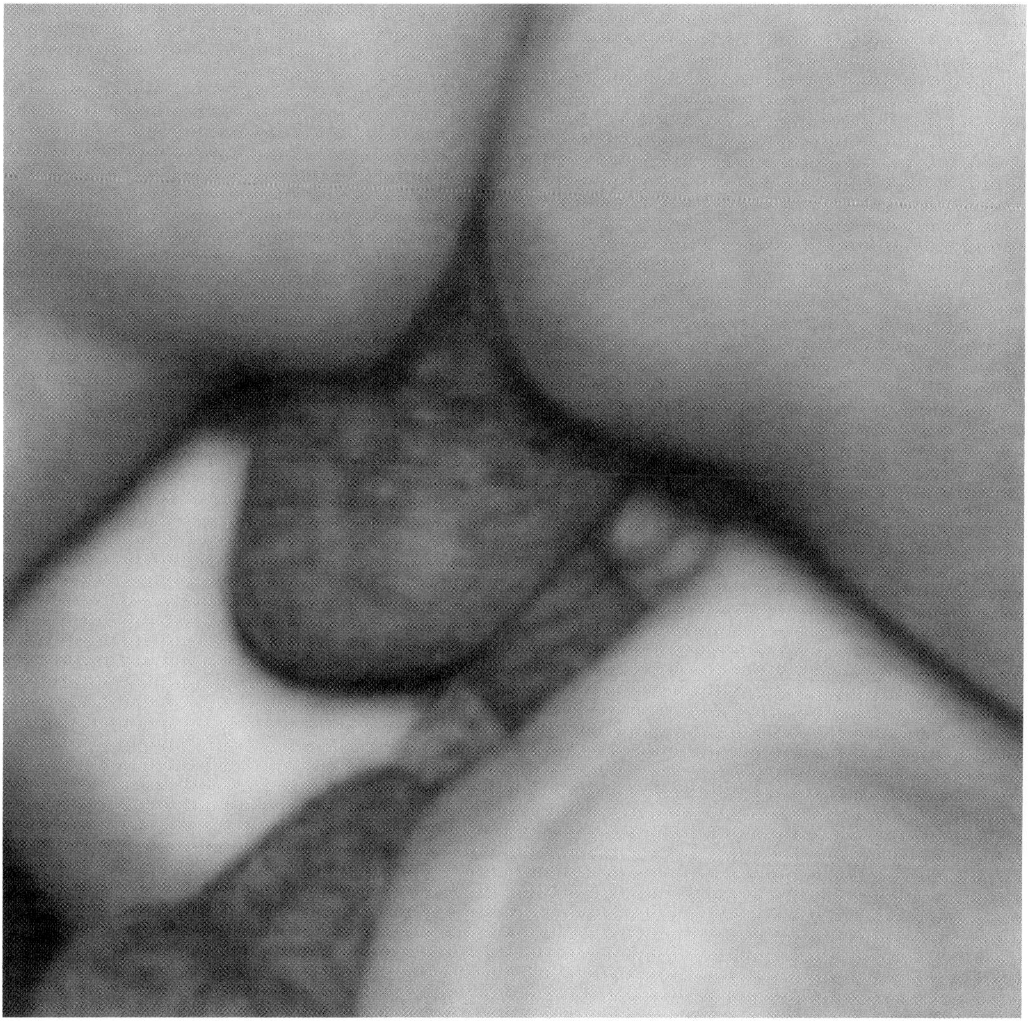

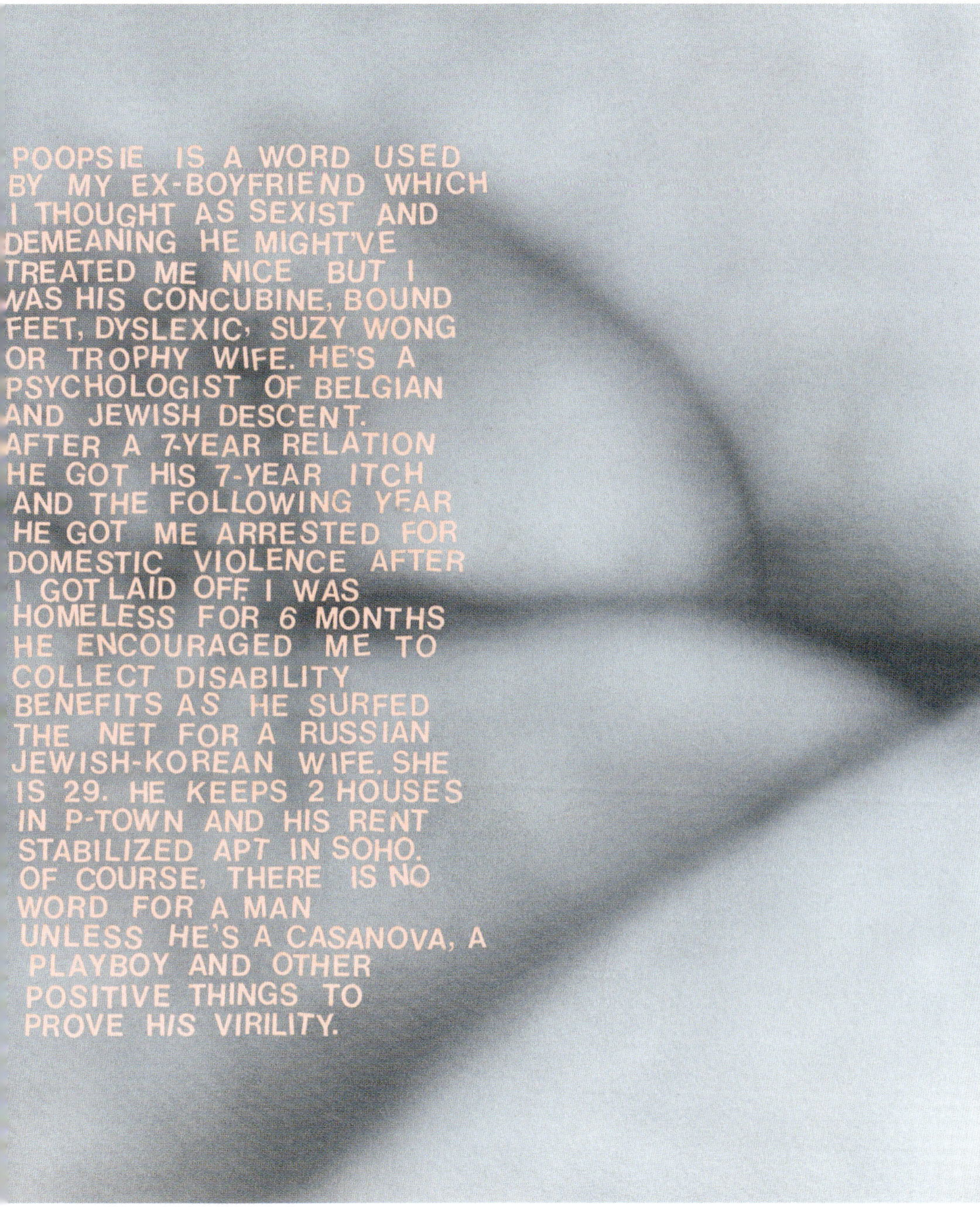
POOPSIE IS A WORD USED
BY MY EX-BOYFRIEND WHICH
I THOUGHT AS SEXIST AND
DEMEANING HE MIGHT'VE
TREATED ME NICE BUT I
WAS HIS CONCUBINE, BOUND
FEET, DYSLEXIC; SUZY WONG
OR TROPHY WIFE. HE'S A
PSYCHOLOGIST OF BELGIAN
AND JEWISH DESCENT.
AFTER A 7-YEAR RELATION
HE GOT HIS 7-YEAR ITCH
AND THE FOLLOWING YEAR
HE GOT ME ARRESTED FOR
DOMESTIC VIOLENCE AFTER
I GOT LAID OFF. I WAS
HOMELESS FOR 6 MONTHS
HE ENCOURAGED ME TO
COLLECT DISABILITY
BENEFITS AS HE SURFED
THE NET FOR A RUSSIAN
JEWISH-KOREAN WIFE. SHE
IS 29. HE KEEPS 2 HOUSES
IN P-TOWN AND HIS RENT
STABILIZED APT IN SOHO.
OF COURSE, THERE IS NO
WORD FOR A MAN
UNLESS HE'S A CASANOVA, A
PLAYBOY AND OTHER
POSITIVE THINGS TO
PROVE HIS VIRILITY.

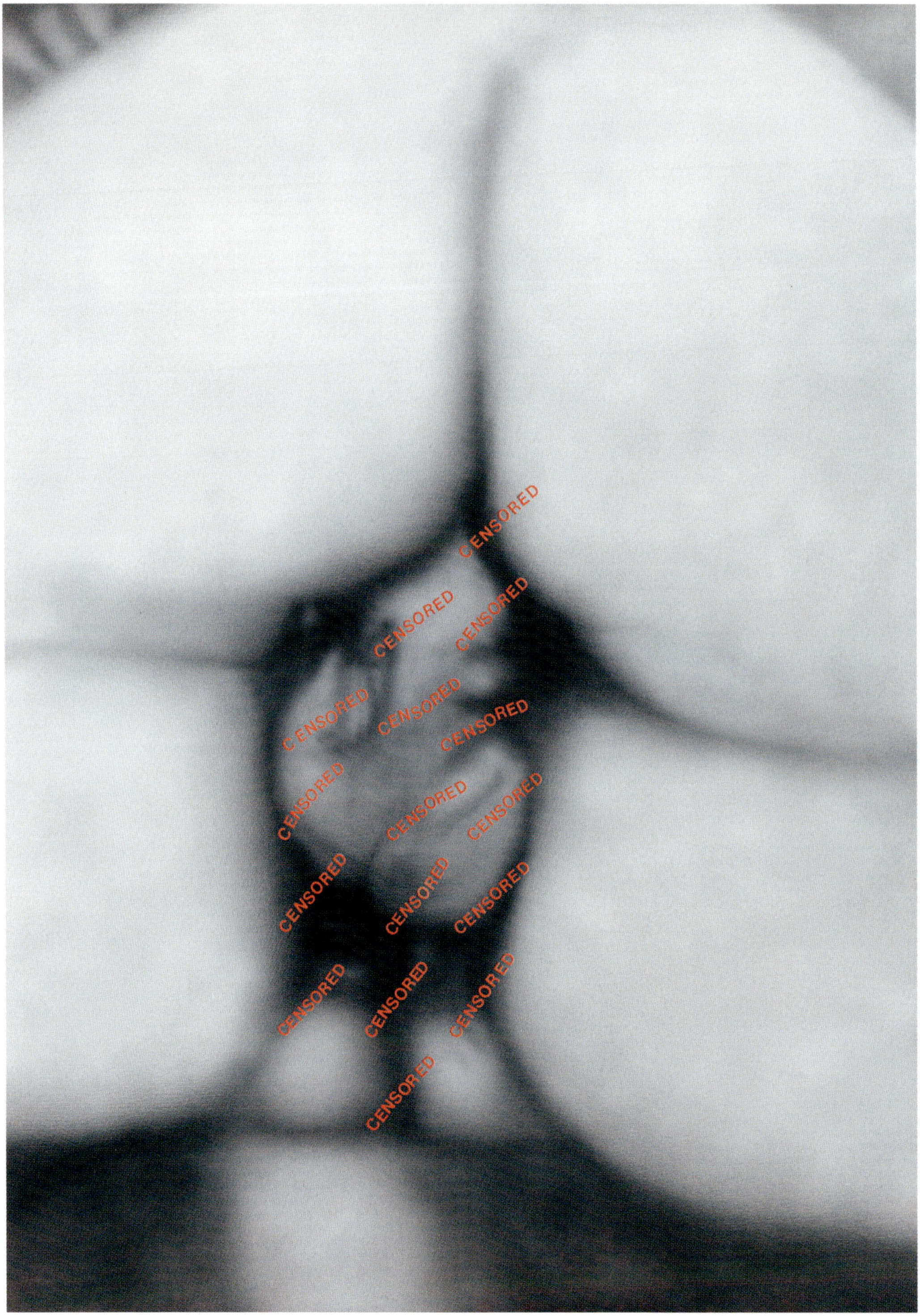
CENSORED
CENSORED
CENSORED
CENSORED
CENSORED
CENSORED
CENSORED
CENSORED
CENSORED
CENSORED
CENSORED
CENSORED
CENSORED
CENSORED
CENSORED
CENSORED

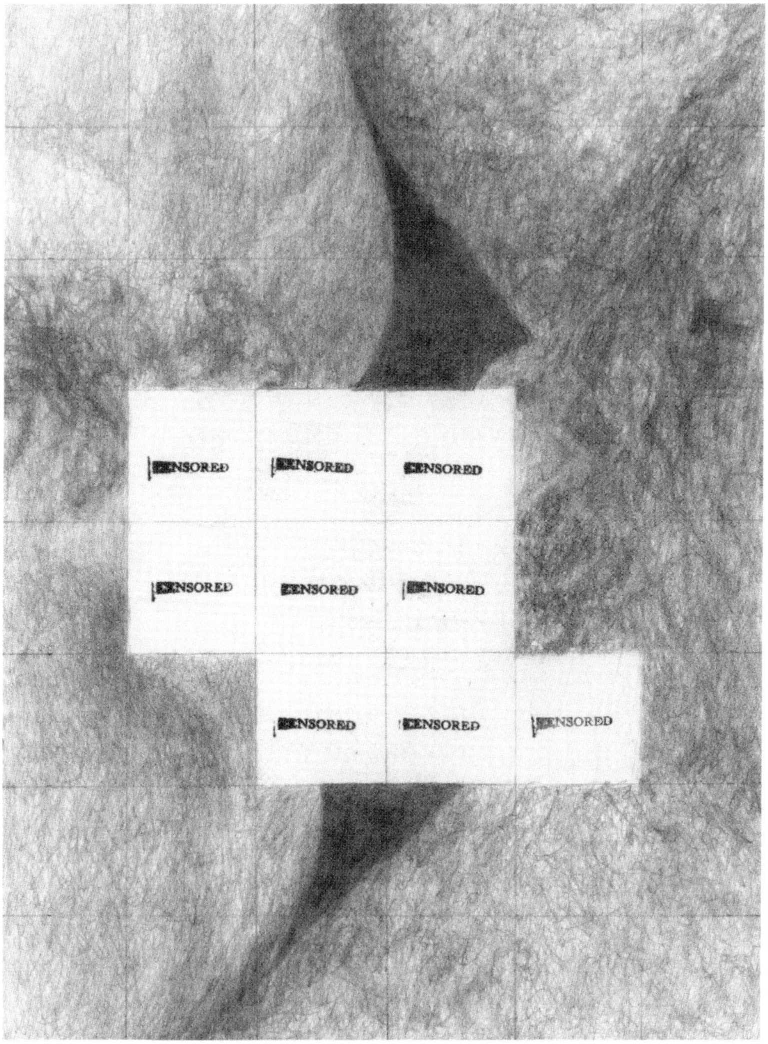
CENSORED
CENSORED
CENSORED
CENSORED
CENSORED
CENSORED
CENSORED
CENSORED
CENSORED

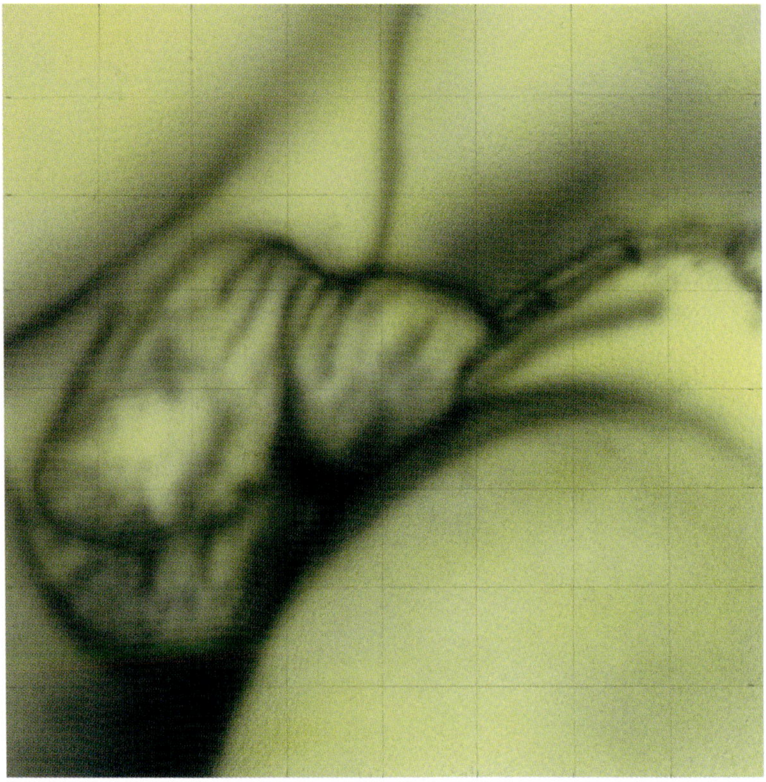

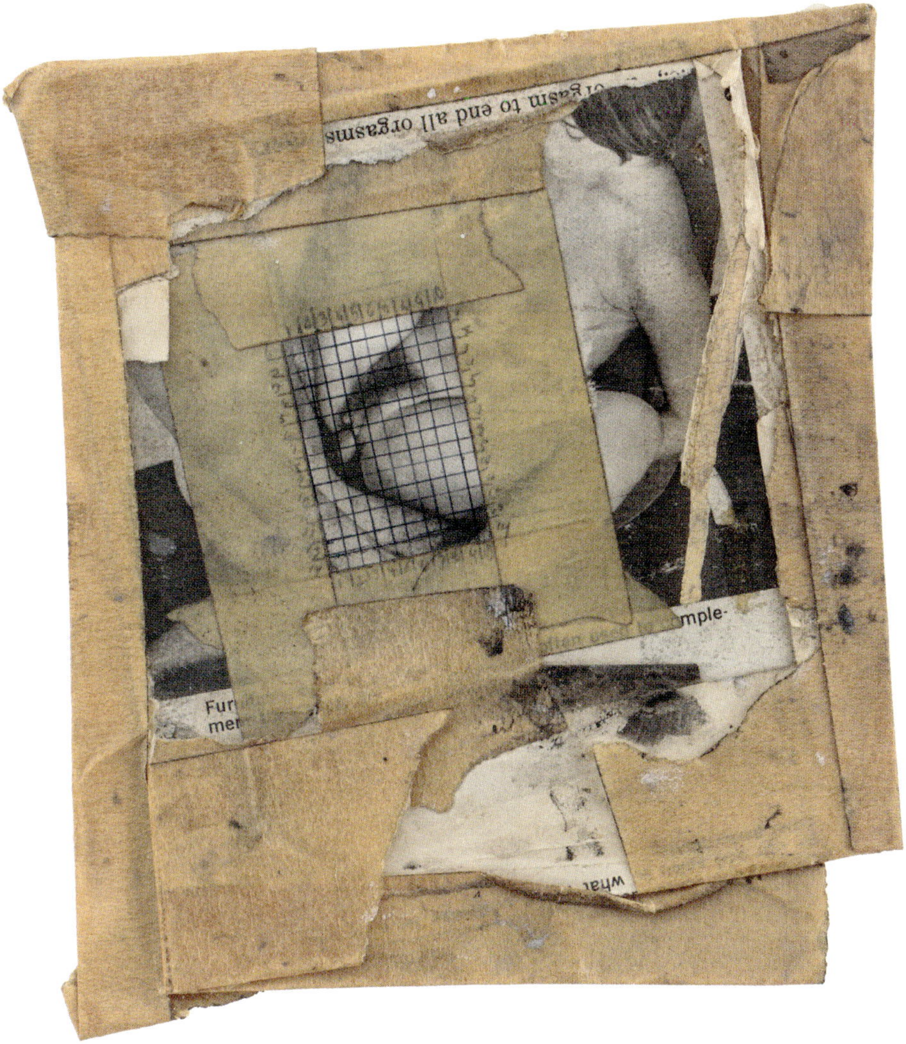
orgasm to end all orgasms
mple-

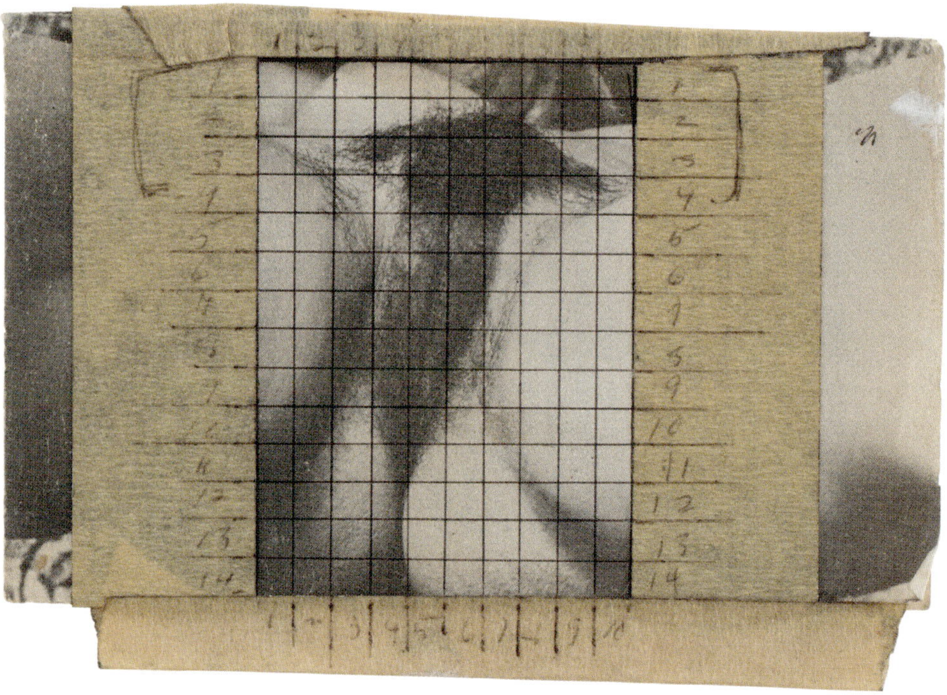

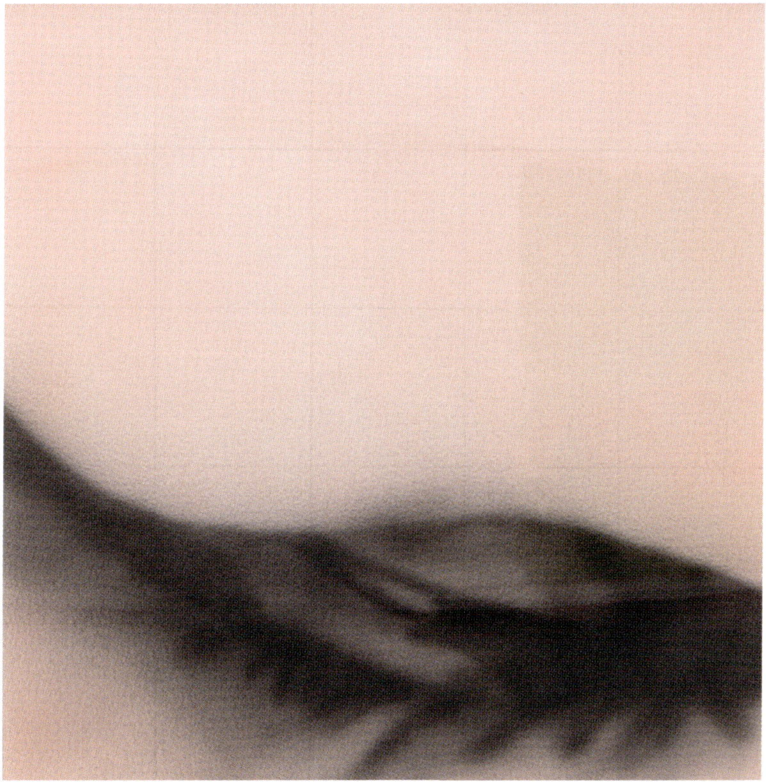

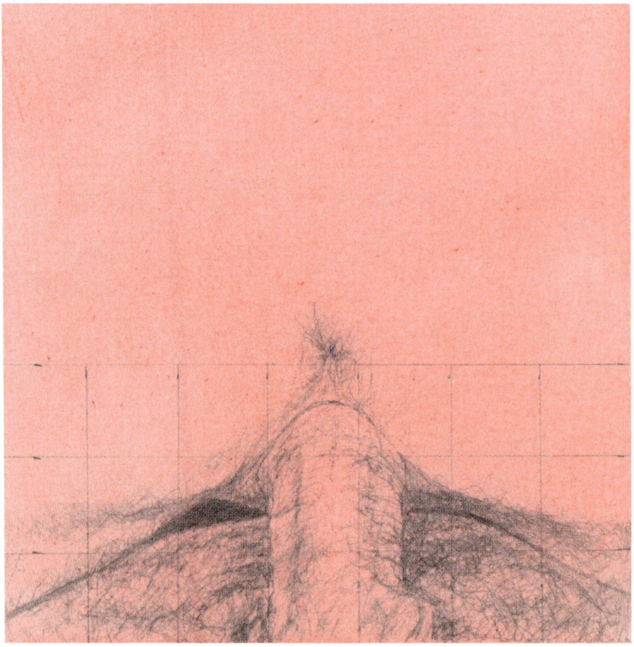

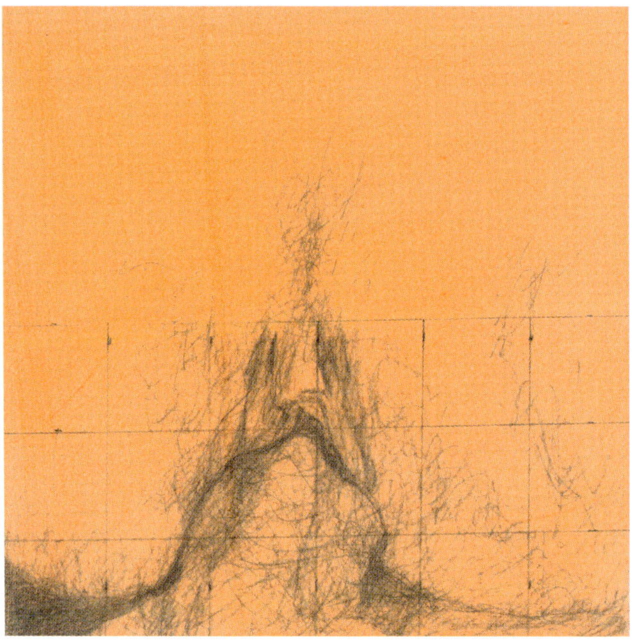

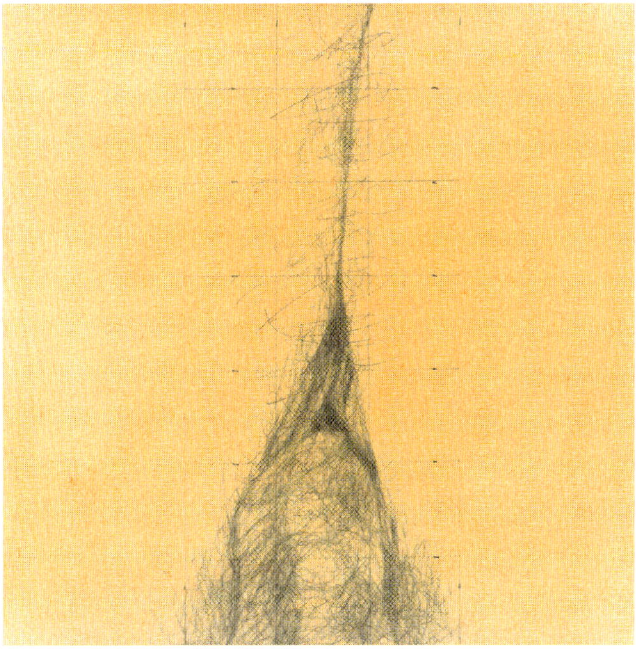

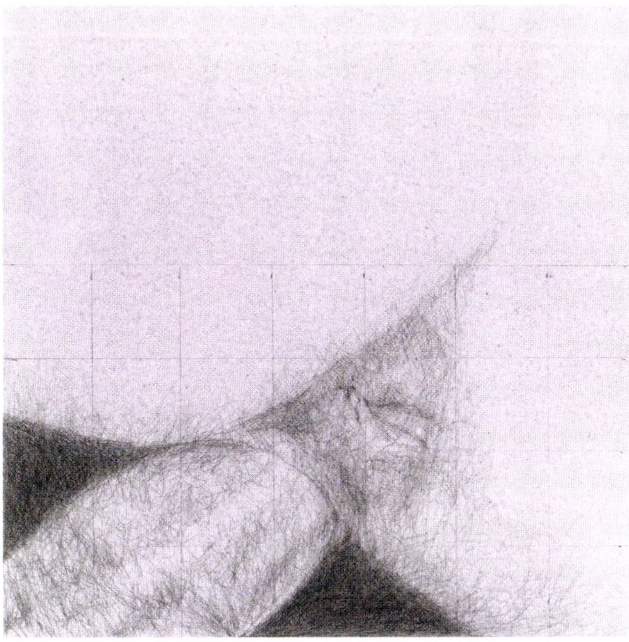

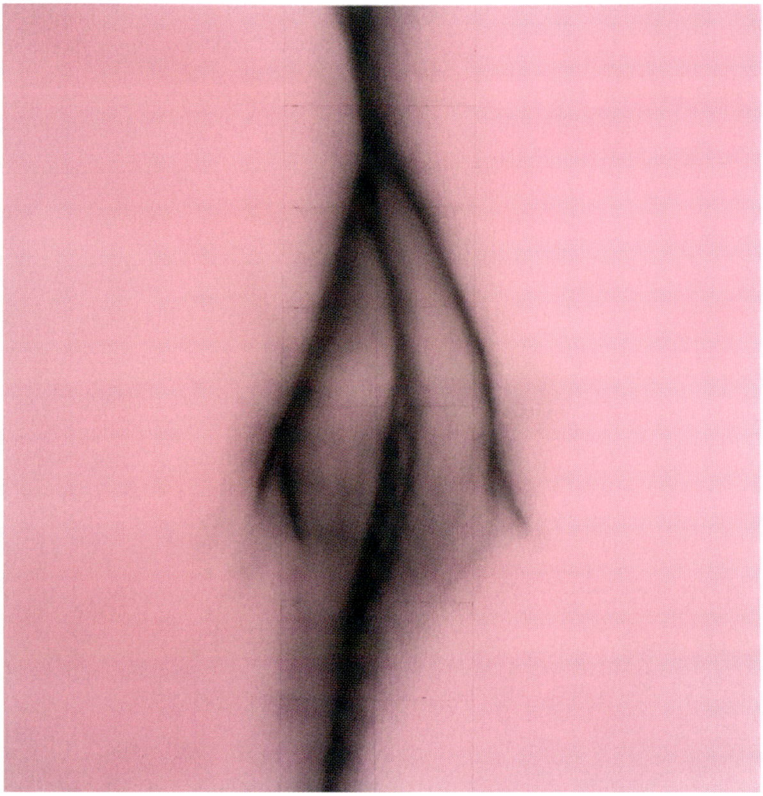

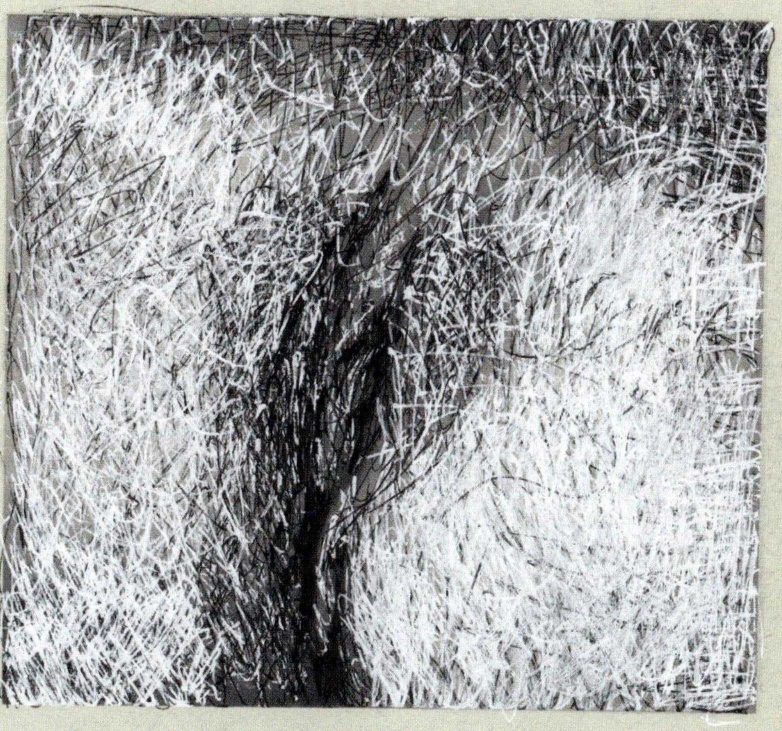

Photo Drawing #5 Betty Tompkins ©2019

Photo Drawing #6 Betty Tompkins ©

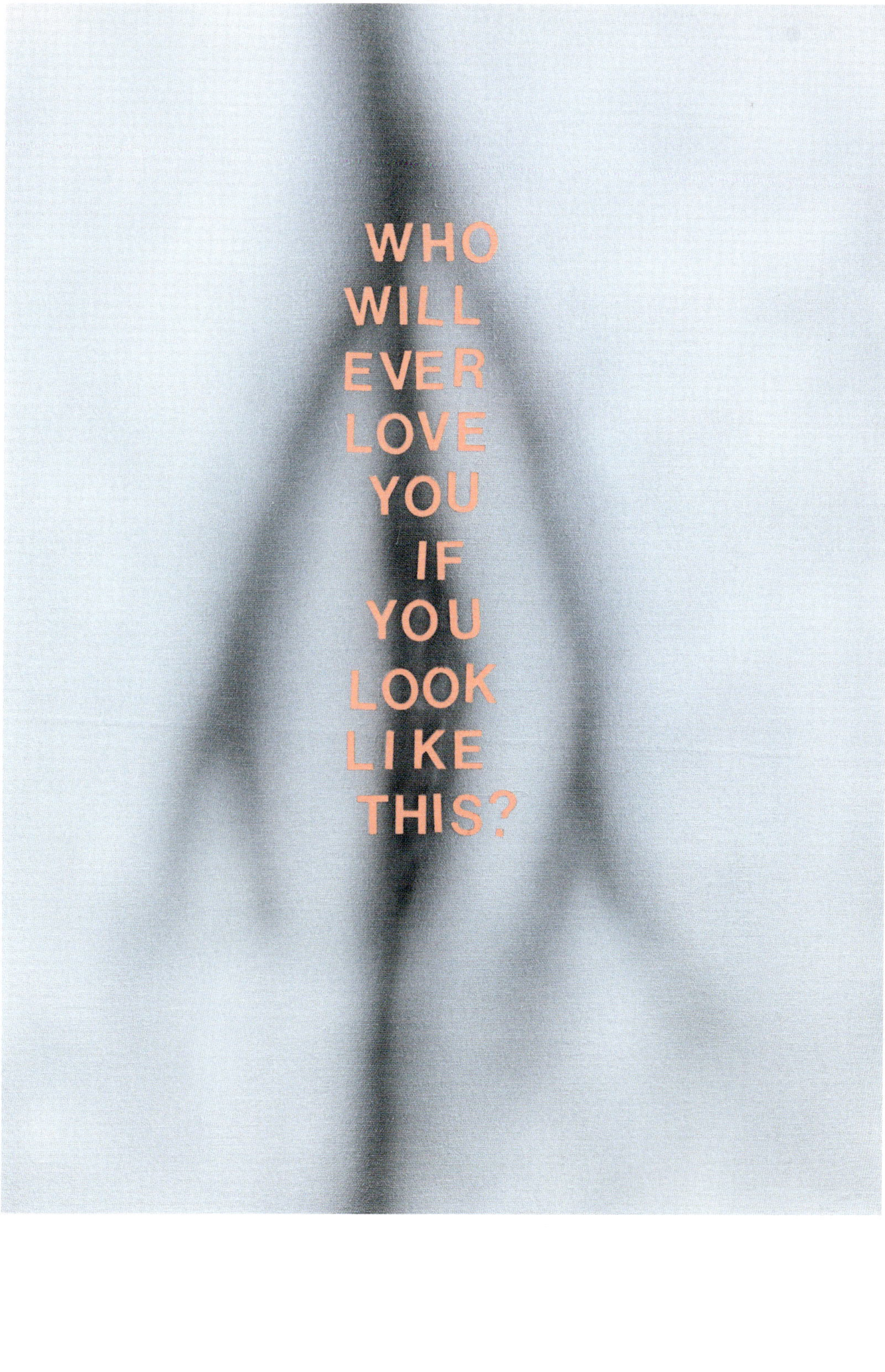
WHO
WILL
EVER
LOVE
YOU
IF
YOU
LOOK
LIKE
THIS?

MY EX'S FAVORITE TERM OF ENDEARMENT FOR ME WAS 'SCLEPROCK,' WHICH HE USED NEARLY DAILY BUT ESPECIALLY WHEN EXPLAINING TO ME WHY GOING BACK TO SCHOOL OR WORK WAS A WASTE OF TIME FOR ME. IT WAS FINE FOR ME TO HAVE 'HOBBIES' LIKE PLAYING AT A CAREER OR SEEKING HIGHER EDUCATION AS LONG AS I REMEMBERED THAT MY REAL JOB WAS TO KEEP HIS HOUSE AND GOOD LUCK TO ME IF I GOT BEHIND ON THE LAUNDRY OR DIDN'T HAVE DINNER ON THE TABLE AT 7PM. HE HAD HOBBIES TOO: TAKING MY PRESCRIPTIONS, SMASHING MY HEAD INTO THE WASHING MACHINE, CHOKING ME UNTIL I PASSED OUT, TAKING MY PHONE AND LAPTOP AWAY AND GENERALLY BEING AN ABUSIVE SHIT. BUT I HAD IT COMING TO ME BECAUSE I WAS JUST A 'SCLEPROCK.'

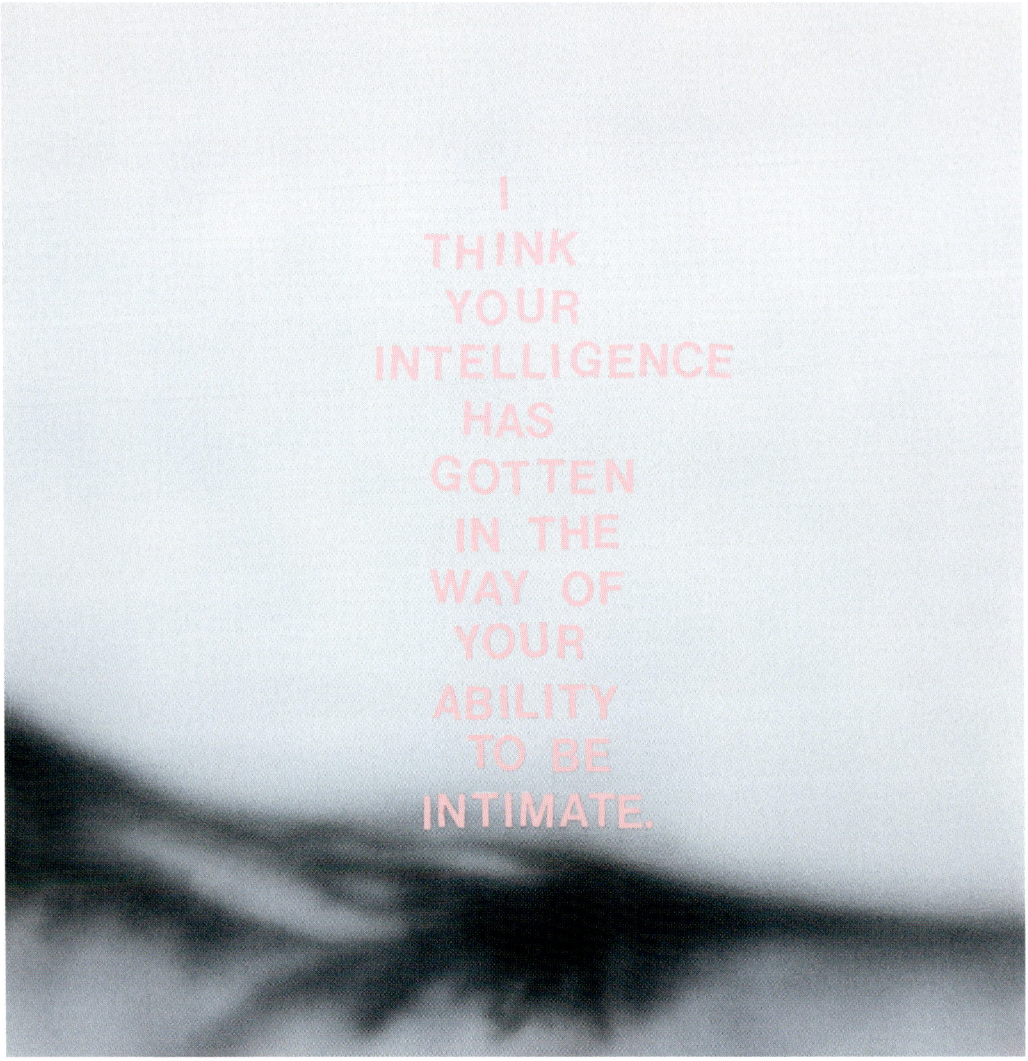
I
THINK
YOUR
INTELLIGENCE
HAS
GOTTEN
IN THE
WAY OF
YOUR
ABILITY
TO BE
INTIMATE.

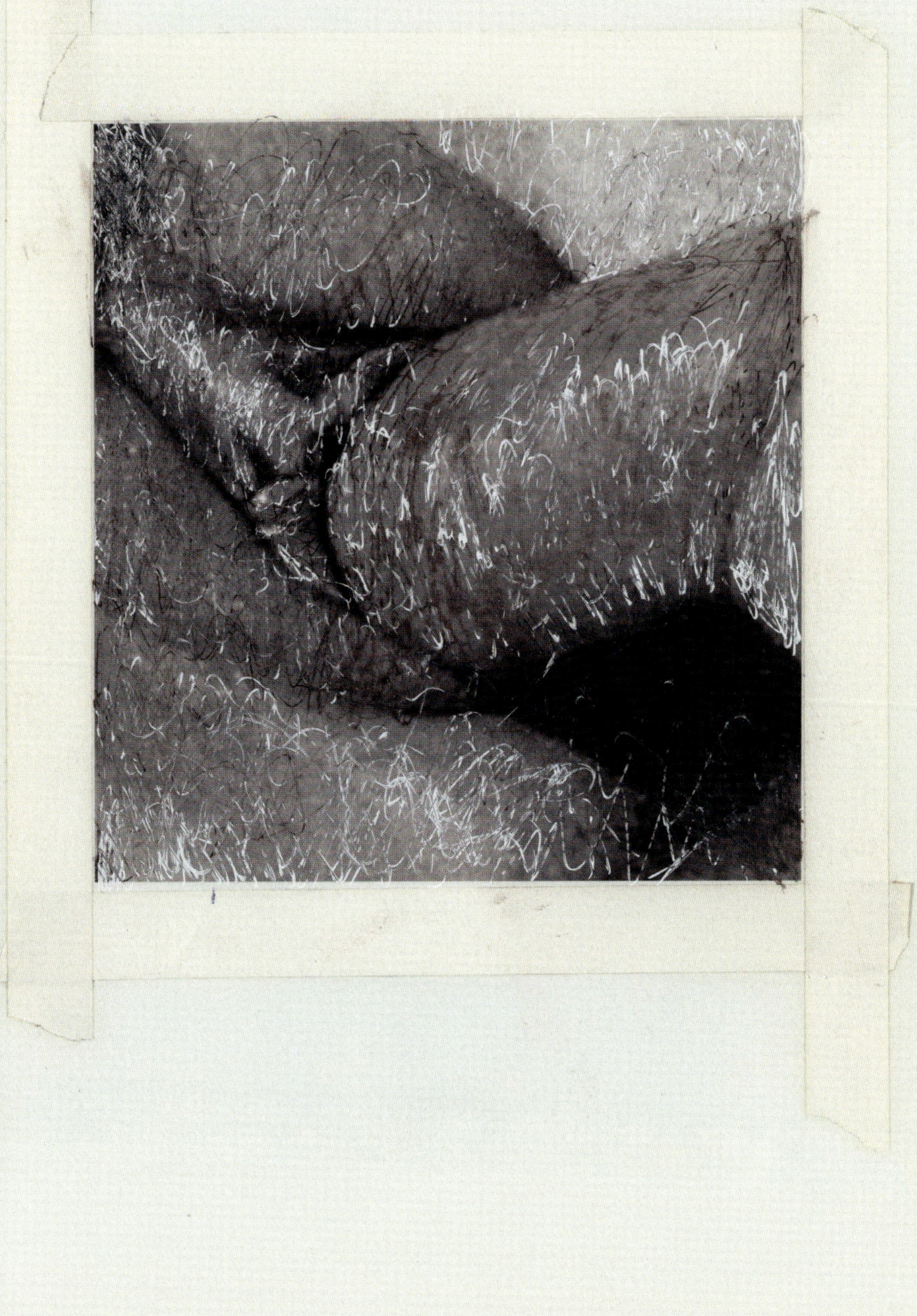

Photo Drawing #9 Betty Tompkins Oct-13

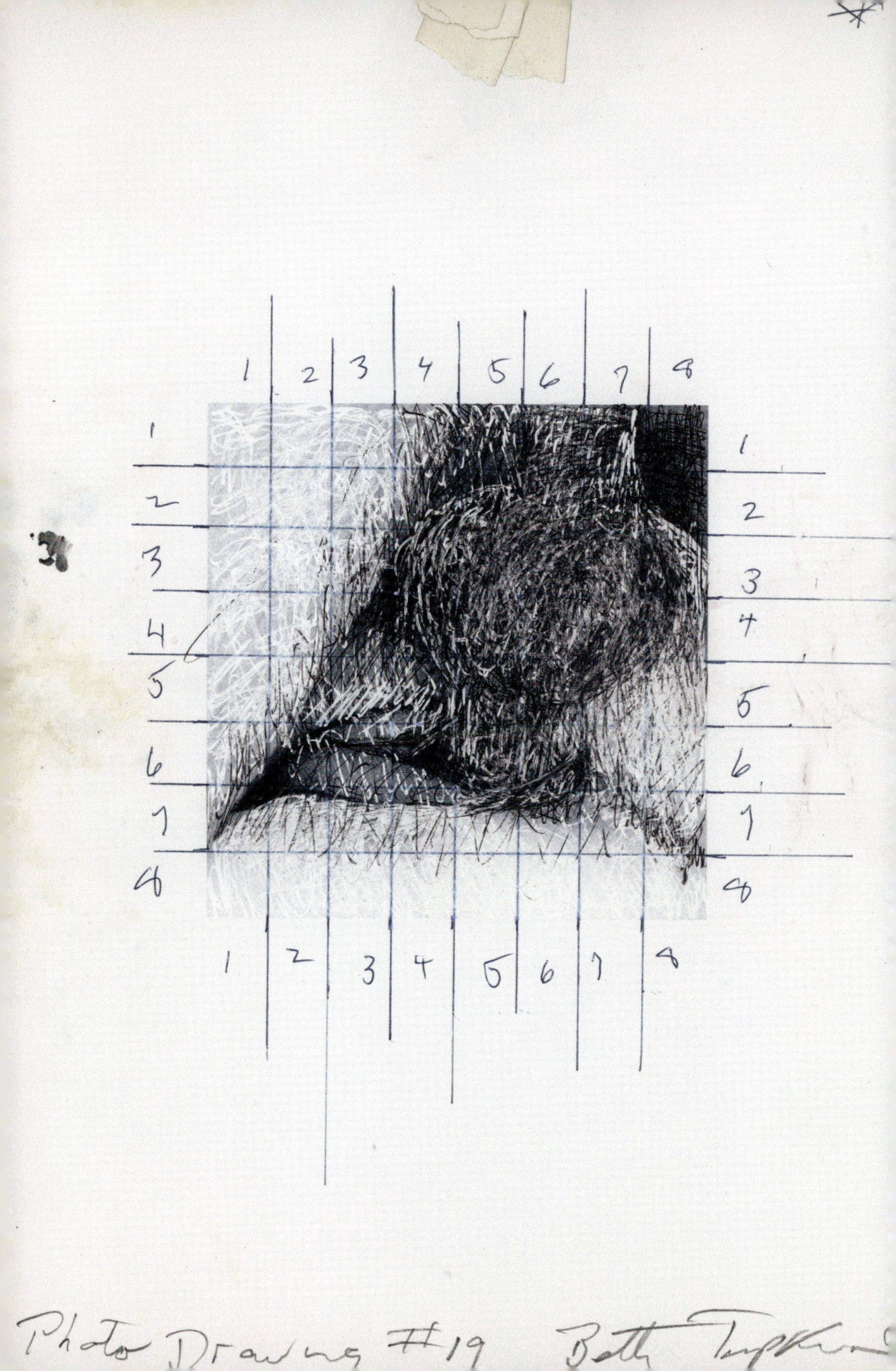
Photo Drawing #19

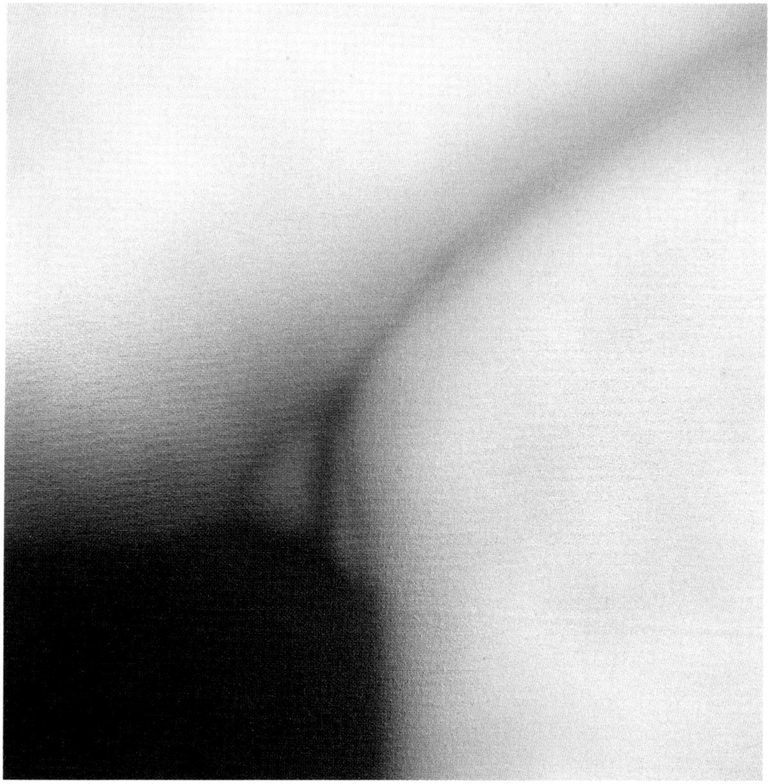

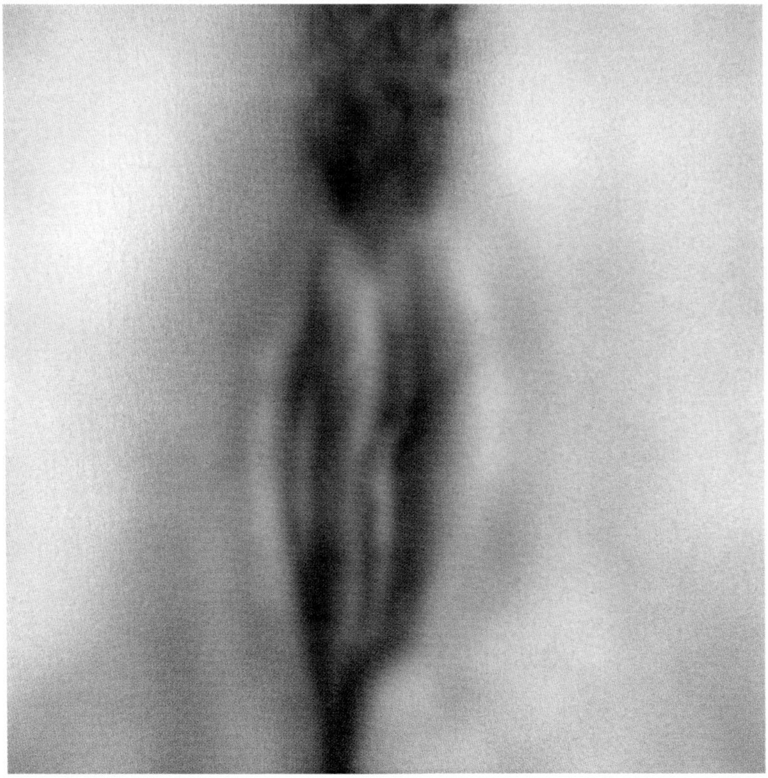

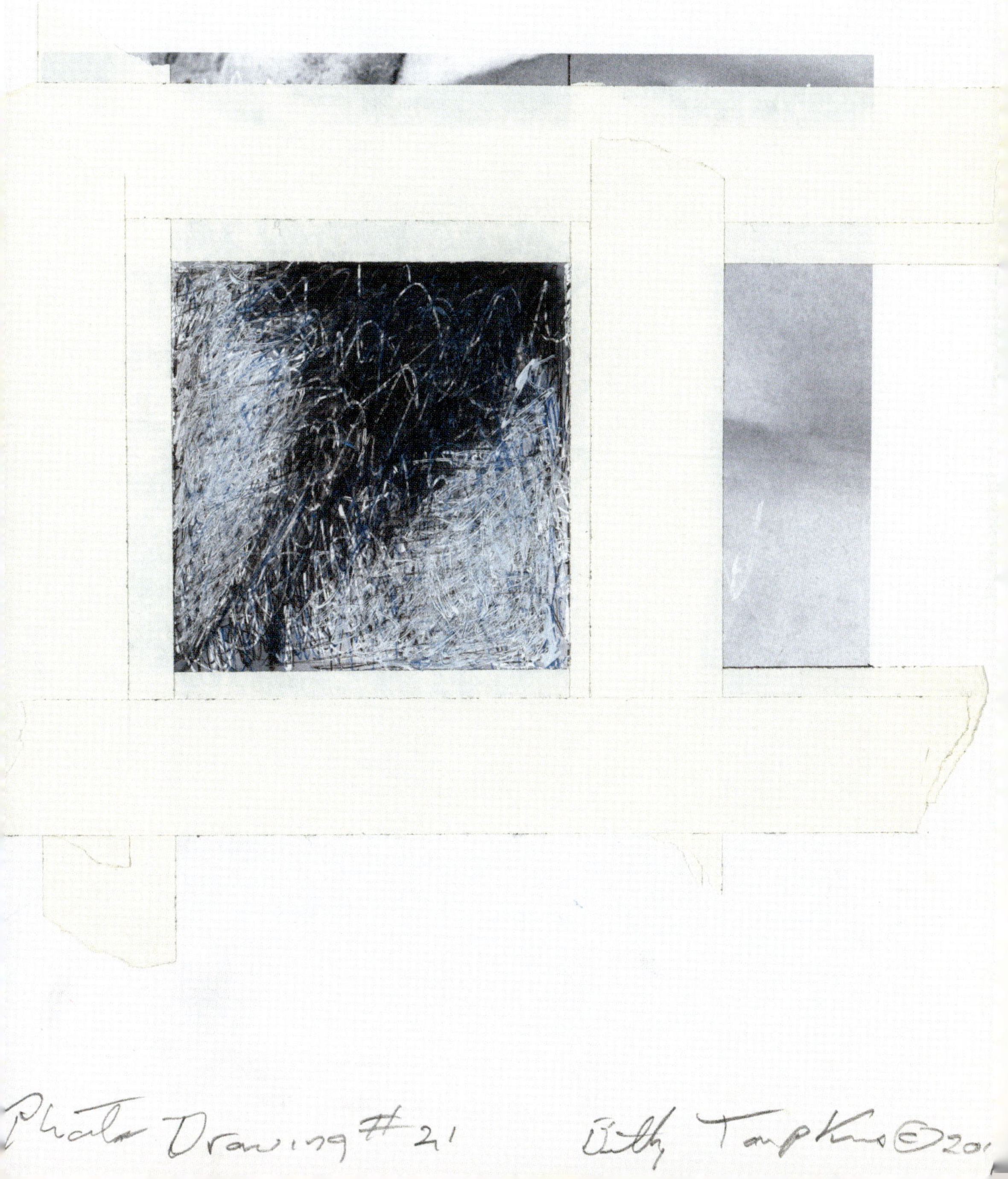
Photo Drawing #21

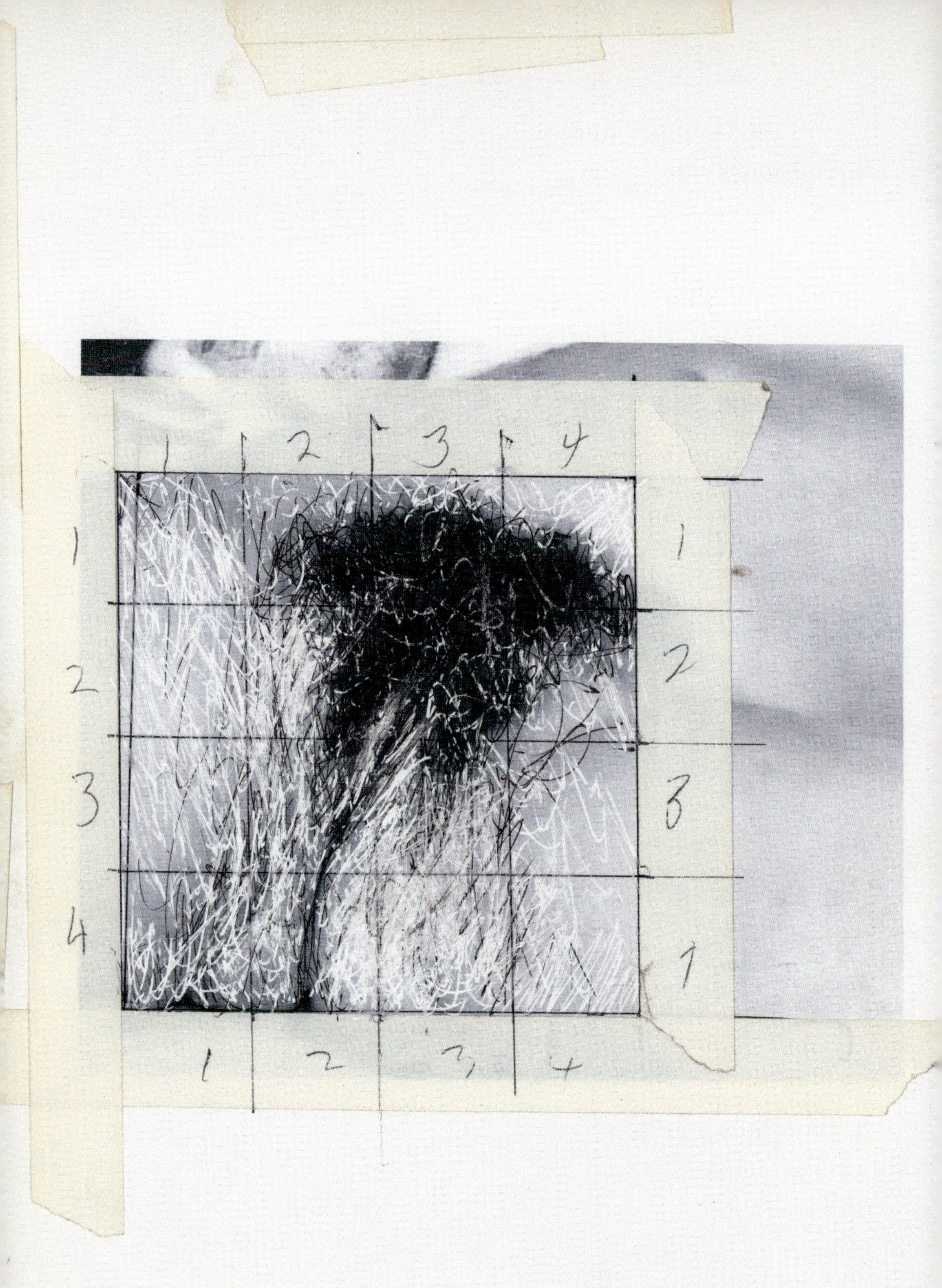

Photo Drawing #13

Betty Tompkins ©

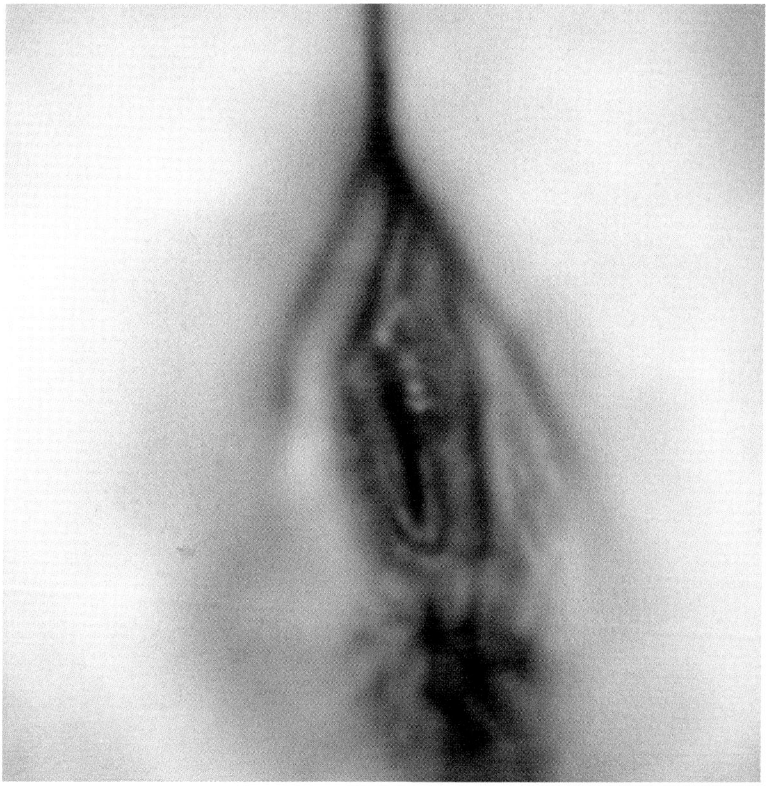

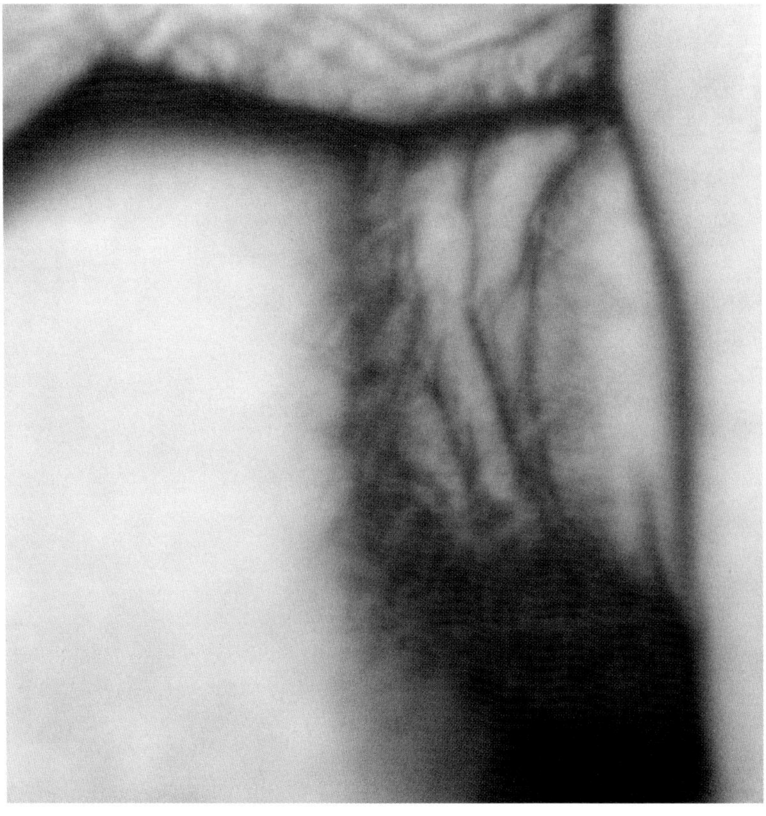

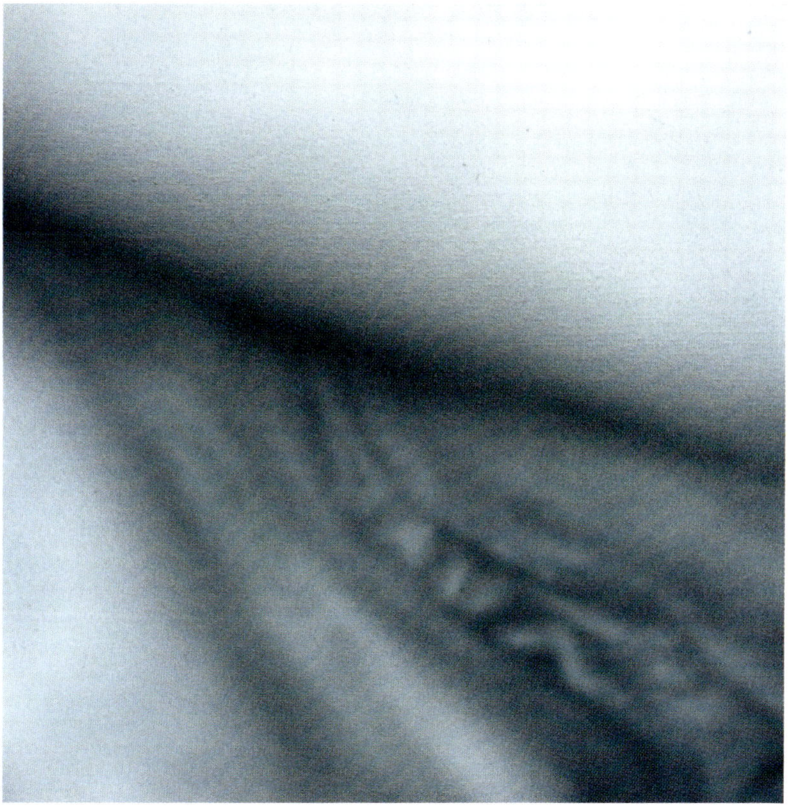

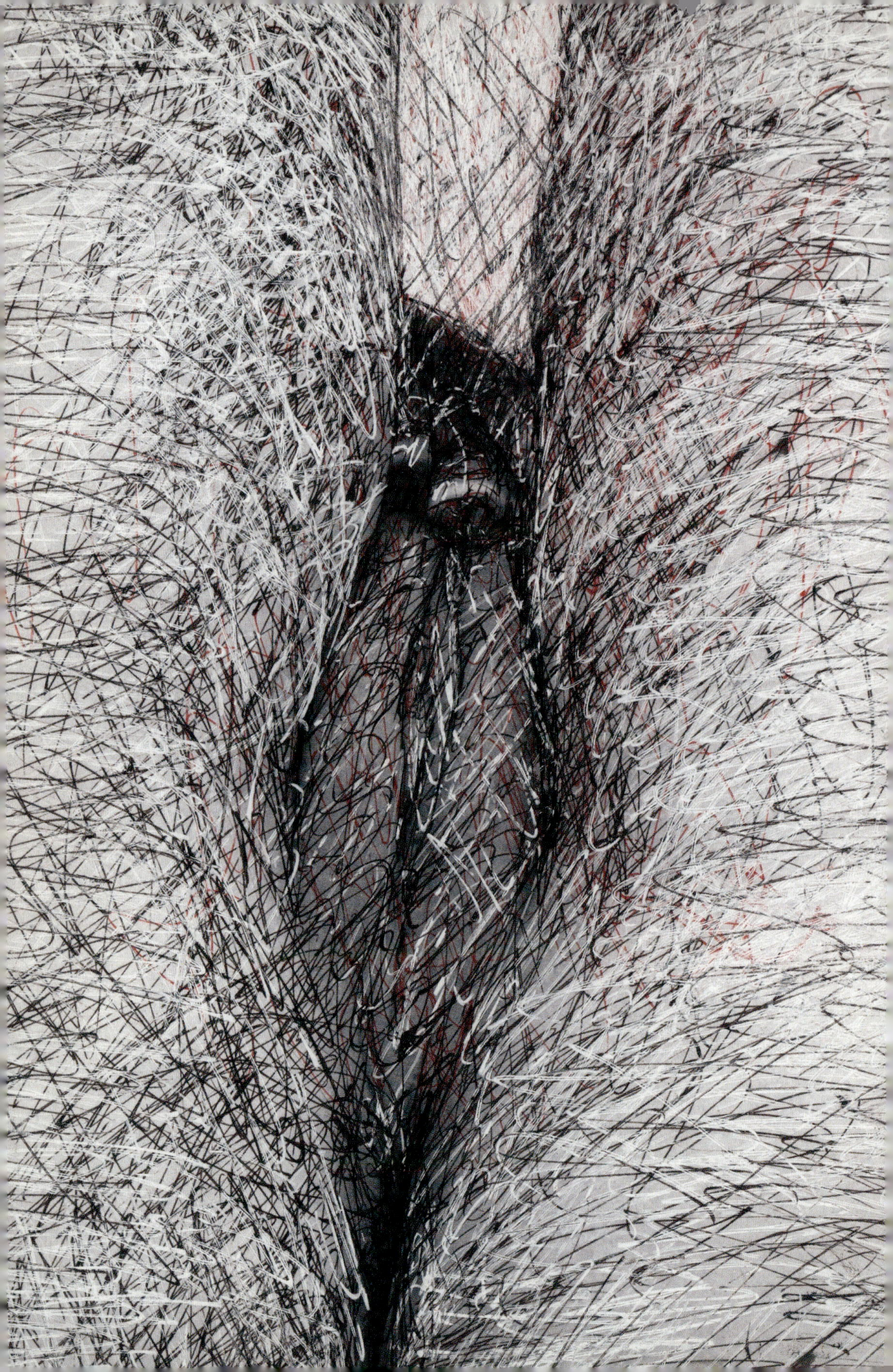

ANYA HARRISON When did you first begin painting?

BETTY TOMPKINS Apart from the usual children's activities, I didn't pick up a paintbrush until I reached high school. In my sophomore year, a friend of mine asked me to come to the art club after school one day to pose for her. When I arrived, she was busy working on something else and told me to occupy myself with some paints. Even though I considered myself stunningly untalented and inadequate for anything visual, I finally got bored of waiting and set up to paint a still life of pots and pans. Interestingly, this turned out to be my very first grisaille painting. I wasn't enthralled by the array of colours that were available, so I began mixing them and came up with all these different shades of grey.

The teacher who led the art club, Gladys Bloch, was an outspoken defender of women artists as it turns out. She came over to me sitting on the floor and asked to see my work. I gave her the board, she called the entire class to her attention and started to talk about my painting, its use of space and mixed colours. I was listening to her, without the faintest idea of what she was talking about, until she finally handed me back the painting with the words, "Art club meets every Wednesday right after school. Be there." She effectively ordered me into the art club, and subsequently I took her classes at school. When I was preparing to apply to art school, I showed her my portfolio and she went through it, shaking her head and saying, "Betty, your drawing is just terrible. But you can learn that. And your colour is god-awful. But you can learn that too." I asked why I was even bothering to apply to art school if my drawing and colour were so bad, to which she responded, "Because you have the one thing that nobody can teach you. You're already an artist, and the rest is all practice." I never forgot those words. It is one of the biggest compliments that I have ever received in my life. Essentially, she was telling me to believe in myself and that I would work something out. It is hard to give a sixteen-year-old that kind of confidence, but she gave it to me. It was a tremendous gift.

AH Who were the painters, or other artists, that you followed during your studies and when you were in the early stages of your practice? Were there particular artists that you studied at school?

BT I was following the art of my time, which means firstly the Abstract Expressionists when I was in college and as a graduate student. Of these, Willem de Kooning was my absolute favourite, closely followed by Hans Hoffman in second place. And everybody else was in third place. Except for Clyfford Still, who I didn't like neither then nor now. I was able to see many of his works in person while I was an undergraduate at Syracuse University, which is close to Buffalo, so I saw a whole lot of Clyfford Stills at the Albright-Knox Gallery which contains 20-30 works in its permanent collection, and I didn't like any of them. They didn't speak to me, there was nothing he was doing with the paint that I could engage with. I found his shapes and forms clichéd. He was the one I truly disliked.

At the same time, it was the early days of Jasper Johns and Robert Rauschenberg, swiftly followed by the Pop artists whom I loved. Looking at their work, it was the first time that I had ever drawn a connection between popular culture and the major ideas that could be drawn out, extracted from it and engaged with.

AH You mention these artists, all of whom are male. At the time, were you aware of female painters like Elaine de Kooning, Helen Frankenthaler, and others?

BT Absolutely, I was very well aware of them. In my second year of college, I had a painting teacher who gave us impromptu, spontaneous lectures. Once, this was in 1963 or 1964, he gave us a three-hour-long lecture on why there were no great women artists. He seemed not to have noticed that the class was three-quarters women. We protested like you wouldn't believe against his old-school point of view. No matter which example of a female artist we brought up, he would always find something uncomplimentary to say about them. I went so far as to accuse him of being blind sighted and said, "You're just blind to what's right in front of you. The only thing that you can tell us about these artists is who their husbands were." One of the artists I had really studied was Lee Krasner, watching documentary films about both her and Jackson Pollock at work, and looking at the chronology in the development of both their practices. She beat him by years. And he stole from *her*. She then dedicated her life to promoting his career because that would put food on the table, while promoting her own would not. I was shocked by that. Yes, I was aware of these artists, but everybody so denied it around me, and I'm glad to see that this now has changed quite a bit.

AH After finishing your studies at Syracuse University you moved to New York City. What was that experience like?

BT When I came to New York in 1969 and started the *Fuck Paintings*, every dealer that I visited would have the same thing to say: "We don't show artists your age. Come back in ten years." However, when you're creating mature work, you know it. It's just a feeling. And I knew these paintings were something. The next thing these dealers would say was, "As a matter of fact, don't come back. We don't show women. We have no market for women." And when pressed, they would confess, "No intention to develop one either, so don't bother." It was actually very liberating for me as it meant I could do whatever I wanted – nobody cared. This was also a period where you were not expected to leave school and immediately walk into a career, which is the case for young artists nowadays.

AH What were you painting before the *Fuck Paintings*? How did your style and choice of subject matter change or evolve?

BT My graduate thesis was on images taken from popular culture. I sourced a lot of images from advertising and from the Sears' catalogue, which came once a year in the post and was a treasure trove of images. I would make paintings from images found in the catalogue.

AH When did you first start using an airbrush, and why the decision to reject the use of traditional brushes and of a direct, physical contact with the canvas?

BT While in graduate school, I made a list of everything that I was very good at with art. I was preparing myself for a lifetime of artmaking and the question I posed myself was: what's the challenge? Once you've mastered the skill of painting, you just bang out the works. I have a very low boredom threshold so I set myself the goal of keeping painting new and fresh, meaning that I would abstain from doing one or two things from the list with each new piece that I began. I did think at the time that I would annihilate painting for myself through this list.

One of the aspects that I loved about painting back in those days was the feel of the brush on the canvas. If you've ever spoken with other painters, they are bound to say the same thing. The brush bounces off the canvas, and the sensation is so pleasurable that you just want to do it all the time. It is physically addictive. Eventually, I reached this line on my list: no more using brushes. As an alternative, I bought a spray gun at a hardware store, one of the large ones which are used to paint a house, and which effectively allow for zero control of application. I armed myself with that, and a huge amount of masking tape, and taught myself how to paint with it.

After moving to New York, my first husband and I lived at Teachers' College Graduate Housing, which is part of Columbia University. It consisted of two rooms, with a kitchen attached to the end of one room, and a bathroom to the end of another. My husband claimed the living room, and I got the bedroom, which held a double bed and a chest of drawers. The bed was about five feet from the window. This was my studio. I spent a lot of time hopping from one side of the bed to the other, and when I no longer wanted to look at art, I would throw all the pillows in the bathtub and lie there reading a book. Given the confined living and working environment, I quickly realised that it wouldn't take long to get lung disease if I kept using the same spray gun. So I bought an H-type single-action airbrush and learned to paint with it. It's what I use to this day. At first, I had huge trouble painting edges, it took me years to master them, so I ended up using a lot of masking tape. This is how I created the first four or five of the *Fuck Paintings*.

AH You have always been very clear about the fact that the choice of subject matter for the *Fuck Paintings* – and the other series that have followed and which have recourse to a sexually explicit iconography – were driven by formal, aesthetic considerations. However, you must also have been conscious of how this imagery may fit, or be rejected by, the dominant feminist discourses of the time, as well as its shock value?

BT I was totally ignorant about the fact that the feminist movement would or could take the position of wholeheartedly rejecting me. In fact, I didn't find out the full extent of their position until a couple of years ago. I was appalled, and to a certain degree I still am. When the feminist movement started in downtown SoHo, I was living uptown close to Columbia, and while I had met a few people associated with the movement, I was not a regular presence in the neighbourhood. In the pre-internet days, information was shared by being out on the street, and the SoHo groups knew each other from restaurants, bars, and walking around in the streets. I would go down to SoHo once a month, but the atmosphere was not so friendly that you could just strike up a conversation with strangers. Plus, I was at least ten years younger than the others, and they were not interested in knowing younger artists. I do think that much of my being rejected or ignored, or both, stemmed from the fact that there was very little opportunity for these women to earn any money, either through academia or gallery sales, so they would only be generous with one or two of their friends, and that was it. The idea of being open-endedly generous had not occurred to anyone.

I appreciated the source images for their formal aspects, certainly, because that is not something that I could manipulate wholly into a composition, but I was also looking for images that had charge. Others since have done the same thing cynically, but for me it was a way of keeping boredom at bay. Let's face it, I was bored silly. More often than not, I would walk into galleries, do a full circle and walk back out the door in two minutes flat, whereas I know the time that goes in to making a painting. It took me a while to realise why I was not spending longer with the work that was then being exhibited, until I came to the conclusion that the paintings looked generic, easy, formulaic. There was no composition, nothing happening with the paint texture, the palette was bland, there were no surprises and the subject matter was dull as shit – so what was I supposed to be looking at? Conversely, if the *Fuck Paintings* had anything, they had charge. I thought that if I turned this image into a painting, and I believed I would do a good painting of it, I would stand in front of it and enjoy it.

AH What informed your decision to work on a monumental scale with the *Fuck Paintings*?

BT The first decision that needs to be made about a painting is its size. I wanted to be big – way bigger than life. I consolidated my decision after seeing some works by Chuck Close, who I knew because he had been one of my husband's college students. He had just finished *Big Nude* and *Self Portrait (with Cigarette)* (both 1967), and I was admiring them in his studio, specifically the way that each square of the grid was like an Abstract Expressionist painting in miniature. Chuck told me that whenever anyone came in and saw the nude, they would always go up to the crotch and measure it with their forearms, which was shocking, because why would anybody do that?! None of these people have a dick that big, so why use your arm? As a result, my first decision about *Fuck Painting #1* was that it should be big: seven by five feet, to be precise. This was the biggest canvas that would fit in to our van at an angle, which is why the first twelve paintings that I made – nine *Fuck Paintings* and three *Cow Cunts* – were all made to this size.

AH Was this decision also made as a way of competing with the male artists of the time, when everyone was working big?

BT I thought that for the paintings to be taken seriously, even though they were not for nearly 40 years, the scale would play an important role.

AH How much time do you spend working on a painting? It is interesting to consider the time aspect in relationship to the source imagery – pornography – which relies on the production of a fast, immediate pleasure.

BT My time is not as splintered anymore. I used to teach six three-hour classes a week at various institutions, so I might only complete two paintings a year. Nowadays, for many reasons, including that I have been doing this continuously every day for several decades, it doesn't take long and I can produce 10-12 paintings a year, as well as a handful of works on paper.

AH Do you paint every day?

BT Yes, except if I'm travelling.

AH In your early paintings, you worked from images that came directly from porn magazines.

BT They were actually porn photos. Porn magazines were murderously hard to get as it was against the law to send them via US Mail. My husband would see the ads in the back of the magazines and he would send in his money order. He had a PO box in Vancouver where he would drive, empty out the box, and hide the envelope in the pillows of his car. They were individual photos, printed using old Kodak processes, and they were tiny, each one measuring around 2 inches by 4 inches. All of my husband's photos were of penetration, but for the *Cow Cunt* paintings I sent him out to get me beaver magazines [which had porn photos just of female genitalia], so the cunts came from there: the money shot.

AH Where do you source your images from now?

BT I source a lot from the Internet and I still send my husband to Times Square with $100. The difference now is that the sellers wrap up three or four magazines together in cellophane, so that you're forced to buy blind. They don't want anybody to go into the shops and start leafing through the magazines, which means that you never know what is going to be inside. I never throw the magazines away because what appeals to me at first glance is not necessarily what I will be interested in one or two years later.

AH While with your early paintings, you were using masking tape to crop in, how do you construct your compositions today?

BT I do everything on Photoshop. I scan everything in, and then I change everything. Everything is up for grabs! I have changed genders, ethnicities, I've exchanged body parts. I mix and match. Some images I can get very quickly, in a day or two, while others take me years to figure out.

AH Let's discuss your choice of colour palette. For the most past, your paintings are notable for their grey tones. Yet there is often an under-wash of colour that can be glimpsed through the grey layers.

BT Quite a lot of my paintings have an under-wash, which refers to an ongoing interest of mine in terms of how the different colour layers affect each other. The paints that I work with have a tendency to be a little bit transparent and translucent. I've used reds, pinks, yellows, blues. They affect the warmness or coolness of the final image, the top layer. When I'm faced with a roomful of my paintings, I can see the difference in the palette. I always mix my own chromatic blacks, I'm currently using a three-colour black, before I used a two-colour one. I do like challenges and problem-solving. I became an artist for the very reason that I could be constantly challenging myself and hovering on the cusp of failure.

AH Why continue to use these grey tones when pornography has long ago left the domain of black-and-white?

BT I used grisaille tones on the early works because those were the tones of the photos, and at that point I was painting exactly what was in front of me. This is no longer of any importance but I keep doing it because it interests me. One of the first things that I do with a scanned image in Photoshop is to drop the colour and take it down to greyscale. I want to see what that will do to the image.

AH What is your process? In the 1970s collages, the grids that you were using to scale the composition on to the canvas are clearly visible. This same grid appears more faintly in the *Grid* drawings and paintings. How do you transfer the original image to canvas, especially given the massive difference in scale?

BT I grid out both the source image and the canvas, and then I work square by square. I have always loved grids because they allow you to isolate information, plus as a practical tool, they're a huge timesaver. Over the years, I have trained myself to look within each individual square and to use its edges for proportion.

After a while, each square acquires its own language. I have a goal of making paintings perfect, so I use the grid because I don't want anyone criticising me for them being anatomically incorrect or off. It's not a discussion that I want to have. Among other things, I don't defend my own work, so I'm loathe to hand out the obvious as criticism.

AH It also makes me think about the relationship in your work between figuration and abstraction, since the grid also has its place in the history of modern art and Minimalism. In her essay "Grids" (1979), the art historian Rosalind Krauss traces this lineage and situates the grid in the interstice between the real and the abstract.

BT That's exactly right. If I think about it, the grid allows me to achieve what I hope I'm doing, which is to be working with abstract and figurative forms simultaneously.

AH Where did the *Cunt* and *Pussy Paintings* originate from?

BT When I returned to the sex subject matter in 2002-03, I wanted to broaden it out beyond the set of rules that I had strictly adhered to with the first *Fuck Paintings* and then the *Cow Cunt* paintings that followed in the mid and late 1970s. This was the moment to do everything: masturbation, kisses, cunts… I wanted to undertake an extended study of what the underpainting did to the overpainting. I bought a number of canvases – all 16 inches by 16 inches – and placed a different colour on each one. I settled on painting images of cunts over them, as they are beautiful images that have a wonderful rhythm to them. After I had painted five or six, I figured out what I needed to, but decided to continue with the series so I've currently completed at least 25 paintings. I called them *Pussy Paintings* in order to avoid confusion with the *Cunt Paintings*, which are painted to a less rigid scale.

AH We have discussed the shock that your representations of sexual intercourse have provoked, and which have led as far as censorship. But have you noticed a difference in the reception of these works from which the male sex is excluded and in which we are instead faced with the female genitalia, in a framework that is more intimate and sensual?

BT A lot of my audience is female, so I imagine they have no trouble with it. However, I still run into problems, for example with the legal departments of magazines who may not necessarily want these images on their website. Plus, there is Instagram, which is notorious and where my account has been taken down twice.

AH Beyond the formal qualities that you draw attention to in your compositions, I feel that there is another type of abstraction at work, in which the human body is transformed into a quasi-landscape with undulations, peaks and troughs. Would this be a fair observation?

BT I have a couple of horizontal paintings which indeed resemble landscapes. I think it's a fair point, and something that carries over from ancient mythology and definitely from Gustave Courbet. One of my *Cunt Paintings* is specifically based on the crotch part of his (not well observed) painting, *The Origin of the World*. I noticed that his model has no outer labia, leading me to conclude that the Realist master did not actually look properly.

AH Why did you pack away your paintings following their censorship and refusal of entry to France in 1973? Did you try to show them following that experience?

BT I definitely tried but my success was at zero. There was no internet, however everyone seemed to know to stay away from me. The only feedback that you could get in those days was in person, through a studio visit, by mail or over the phone, and I just couldn't get it. I never told anyone that I had been censored in Paris, but they all knew to stay away, and to this day I don't know how or why. Now we handle censorship differently, more or less as a point of pride against the prudishness of the internet and social media platforms, but it was a different case back then. Am I surprised to still be censored? No, because it's happened so fucking often. I don't have a huge capacity for shock in that sense. Do I think that I have it coming to me because of what I post? No, because I've read Instagram's guidelines, and they don't even obey them themselves. It's fine to post a mastectomy scar, for example, although I have never seen anybody do that. The following rule is that photographs of nudity in painting and sculpture are allowed. In the meantime, Instagram has its 'review teams', so there is somebody out there who is looking at everything that I post – since I've been censored more times than I can count – and ultimately it's their decision. Someone who I know works there and once told me that the reviewer could not tell the difference between my painting and a photograph, which is probably the first time in my life that I've been in trouble for doing it too well.

AH What were you doing between 1973 and 2002?

BT I never stopped painting. I showed when I could. I tried every three to five years to show the *Fuck Paintings* but nobody would take them. Finally, Jerry Saltz gave Mitchell Algus my set of slides with those paintings on them, which is not something he ever does. Apparently, he brought them to Mitchell, said that he should take a look at the work, put the slides on his desk and left. I got a call from Mitchell saying he was looking at some of my slides from the 1970s, and that he would like to come down and look at the work in person. As my first language pieces also date from the 1970s, I didn't know which works he was referring to. I had some of the *Fuck Paintings* stretched up, but I showed him the word paintings first. He then turned to the *Fuck Paintings* and *Cow Cunts* I had out and said, "That's what I came down for." He wouldn't tell me at first how he got the sheet of slides – I had been sending out the same sheet to everyone – but eventually he told me that they had come from Jerry. I said to him without any hesitation, "I just have to tell you, I don't know Jerry Saltz. I've never met Jerry Saltz, and if you think this is going to get you a review by Jerry Saltz – I don't think so." It was a hilarious conversation. Mitchell wanted to put me in a group show and said he would call to make the final arrangements. I kept waiting for that call, which never came, and finally left him a message on the gallery answering machine. He called me back and explained that the show was off, but that he would like to mount a solo exhibition of my paintings. Mitchell has a terrific reputation. He is a re-discoverer. Artists who didn't get their due the first time around, that's who he shows. At the time he was also teaching so had a basic income and did not have the pressure of making sales. We prepared the show in two weeks flat, including getting the paintings on stretchers, having the drawings framed and producing the announcement, which is the photo of me in Ellensburg [Washington] in 1973, where I'm photographed standing between the two *Fuck Paintings*, and which I had saved during all these years.

AH What was the starting point for the *Insults and Laments* series? What role does language – which we could term another form of abstraction – play in your work?

BT Language plays a huge part in my practice. It turns out that when you take those right-brain, left-brain tests, I'm dead centre. Back in the 1970s and 1980s, once I had finished with the *Cow Cunts*, I had made numerous language paintings and drawings of cows, horses, the sea, the law... With these later pieces, it started in 2002 when I became tired of being alone in my studio all the time. I sent out an email to my contact list, which explained that I wanted to embark on another series using language, but this time about women. In response, I received 1,500 words and phrases, which I saved as I had an idea about what I was going to do, but no form for it yet. In 2013 I sent out the same email, but this time promised anonymity, and this time I received not only an additional 1,500 words and phrases, but stories too, which I settled on applying to canvas as paintings. These are the works that make up *WOMEN Words, Phrases, and Stories*.

In my exhibition at FLAG Art Foundation in New York in 2016, and the ones that followed at Gavlak Gallery in Los Angeles and Palm Beach, we set up all three places so that there was always a wall available with index cards, push pins and markers for visitors to add their own vocabulary, that the exhibition spaces sent to me afterwards. I put off unwrapping them for a long time, and once I did, I was stunned. They were more amazing and shocking than the originals: "I'm going to Jackson Pollock all over your face," or "I blew my load in her face but it was OK because she was a slut." I couldn't let them lie unused, so I decided to make paintings using cunt images. I had completed three or four before I realised that these were all insults or laments, which is what gave the series its name, and it's one that I'm still working on.

AH You paint and repaint the same images over and over again. Because you've been painting them for so long, has their meaning changed for you with time?

BT Yes and no… Yes, simply because I'm older so everything has a different meaning to me now. And no, because my visceral reaction and desire to do the paintings remains as it always has. I have a deep-seated conviction that I find something new in the image to be working with. I crop it differently; I use different materials or colours. To me, it's always fresh and new. Otherwise, it would just be a production line, and I don't do production.

AH What is your relationship to humour? I'm thinking particularly in relationship to your text paintings, which often elicit laughter despite or because of the crassness of their language. I also can't help but imagine you having fun, perhaps having a wry laugh to yourself, while in the process of painting them.

BT I have a wicked sense of humour! I would term my work 'serious humour'. I think it's present in much of my work, never on purpose, because if you're funny on purpose then you're rarely, truly funny. Unless you're Joan Rivers. It's there also as a balance to people's reactions when they see my work: some laugh, some are horrified, some even cover their crotches.

AH How does drawing sit alongside your painting practice? The *Grid Drawings*, for one, often look like preparatory sketches for the paintings. Yet when we were in your studio in New York, you explained that the drawings are finished works in their own right but that they are made post-factum, after the paintings. There seems to be a levelling, if not reversal, of hierarchies there.

BT I've sometimes worked on them simultaneously, but privileging the painting first because otherwise there would be nothing to solve. More often, I do the drawing way after I have finished the painting because I think I can find something else in the image. If I can see the drawing, and I've just experienced the act of drawing, there is no problem to solve and I no longer have a reason to create the painting. I already know where the difficult bits lie. I draw simply because I love to draw. It's a break and since my drawing technique has evolved over the years, I no longer draw so much as I scribble. I once asked myself whether I scribble to ensure that no line is ever responsible for the image, and I think that's very close to the truth. No one can ever say, "This line is responsible for me seeing this dick." It's all a bunch of scribbles so actually you have no idea where one ends and one begins.

AH Are you a feminist? And what does that term mean for you?

BT As opposed to a misogynist, of course! I was raised to believe that I was as good as anybody else. I went to an all girls' high school, which was the smartest decision that I ever made because it consolidated that conviction. The idea that people could think that I wasn't as good as everybody else was a big shock to me. I got a full dose of it when I was in college and the years that followed. What it means to me simply is that all women are as equal as all men, and should be treated as such. Today being the day that Harvey Weinstein has been sentenced to 23 years in prison is a good day to say that. Never have my ideas as an artist been so much in sync with events in wider society than in the period since #MeToo. We've talked about being of your time, and my stance is that you can only ever be of your time, and it's much more pleasant to be accepted for it than rejected. And I would, and have, called my work feminist.

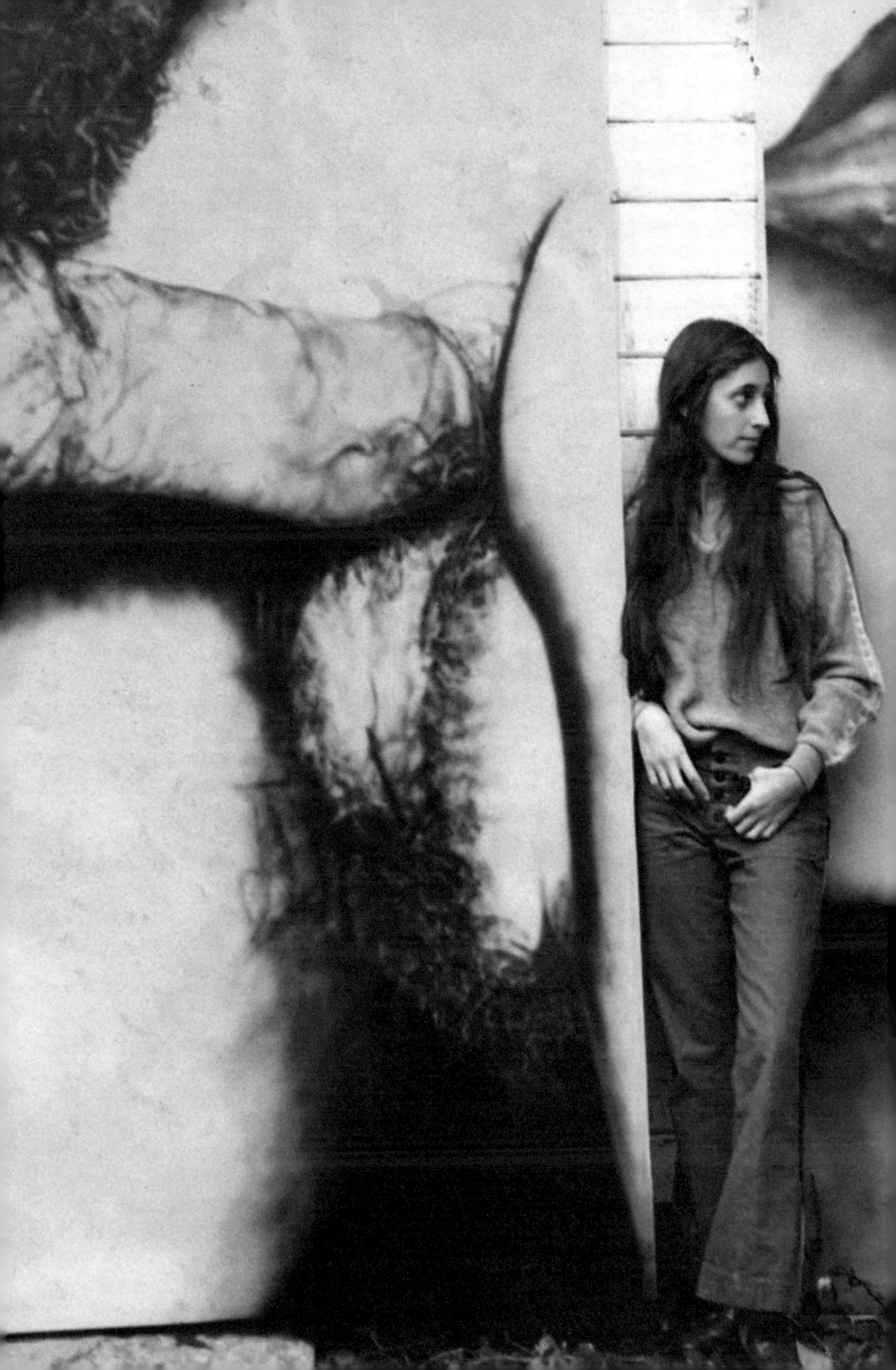

FUCK PAINTINGS: RADICAL PASSIVITY, VISUAL PLEASURE, AND QUEERNESS

GÉRALDINE GOURBE

"And when you're a star, they let you do it [...]. Grab 'em by the pussy. You can do anything."
Donald Trump

"'bitch' serves the social function of isolating and discrediting a class of people who do not conform to the socially accepted patterns of behavior."
Jo Freeman, *The Bitch Manifesto*

Between 1969 and 1974, the young artist Betty Tompkins painted monumental scenes of sexual penetration in hyperrealist detail. She appears between her two large *Fuck Paintings*, with long hair and a frail adultescent body, her gaze fixed on a point out of shot. With one foot in front of the other and her thumbs artfully hooked in the pockets of her jeans, this shy woman appears to be trying to look cool. While searching for a gallery, Tompkins followed the usual distribution channels for artwork. She believed it essential to forge an identity before launching herself into the art market. Each slide presentation that the artist sent to gallerists was completed by a copy of this photo. However, the portrait of the young artist as a painter did not achieve the desired impact – quite the reverse: her *Fuck Paintings* were greeted with indifference in New York art circles.

Decades later, the art critic Jerry Saltz exhumed this portrait from the archives to show it to gallerist Mitchell Algus. After seeing it, Algus gave Betty Tompkins her first solo show in 2002. In the intervening period, the artist had endured invisibility, resulting in several long years of isolation and the seizure of two *Fuck Paintings* by French customs officials in 1973 on censorship grounds.

Betty Tompkins *Ellensburg, WA 1973*, 1973/2013

Radical passivity

This portrait still carries with it an affirmative statement akin to a manifesto. It proudly displays a powerful desire for emancipation from patriarchal visual conventions. The literal nature of its content – i.e. "fucking in painting" or "fuck paintings" robustly challenges us. The manner in which this young woman embraces the subject in this oversize format, and her realistic depiction suggestive of Courbet's *The Origin of the World*, are major contributing factors. By revealing her rejection of feminist theory or a conceptual approach, Betty Tompkins has contributed to what I would term a "radical passivity". Her pictorial choices are guided by the power of abstraction: "I was coming out of Abstract Expressionism. That was my first love as a painter. I wanted to paint something that was abstractly and formally beautiful and
1 challenging and varied."[1]

1 'Beyond the F Word: an interview with Betty Tompkins' in *Art in America*, February 2016 https://www.artnews.com/art-in-america/interviews/beyond-the-f-word-an-interview-with-betty-tompkins-56446/

Her pornographic source material was chosen and reframed for its ability to empower form and trigger a scopic drive in others which makes it impossible to avert one's gaze. In short, we are forcefully compelled to look. The aim of this radicality is not to denounce a patriarchal culture in the manner of certain US West Coast feminist artists such as Judy Chicago, Miriam Shapiro, Faith Wilding, and Suzanne Lacy, with their iconographic world of "cunt art". In contrast to this feminist aesthetic, Tompkins' approach has been interpreted by some feminists as passive or corrupted, a point to which I will return. Moreover, her painting does not attempt to express a feeling. Her research had convinced her that pop artists' obsession with "seeing" had destroyed the romantic illusion of the abstract expressionists. Her *Fuck Paintings* are all the more scandalous because they reveal a sexuality devoid of emotion.

Betty Tompkins unwittingly stands at the crossroads of different movements. Although she learned a great deal from pop art painting, she has never actually considered herself to be a pop artist. She has admired certain abstract expressionists, but her work post-dates them historically. While it is true that she shared the aspirations of a whole host of women artists living in New York who were interested in depictions of sexual pleasure, she steered clear of the political culture of this group: "I am free of theory, which I consider a blessing, to tell you the truth. My impression over the years was that you had to go to the consciousness-raising
2 meetings and read the books. I read a lot of material on my own."[2]

2 Idem.

Looking at Betty Tompkins' career with the benefit of hindsight, we can observe the absence of any inscription or territorialisation, although this was not a particularly deliberate move on her part. Tompkins' non-identification is a recurring theme in her writings.

This has led to isolation, but has also afforded her a degree of latitude. This involuntary passivity, which forms part of the context of the production of the *Fuck Paintings*, is coupled with a radicality which can be measured against the yardstick of this era characterised by contradictory waves that helped shape the cultural and artistic transition from pop to conceptual art, and the eruption of feminist, Marxist, homosexual, and anti-militarist activist thinking.

An understanding of this dynamic provides an insight into why and how the *Fuck Paintings* were out of step with their time then, but are much less so now.

Visual Pleasure: Between Pop Art and Conceptual Art

With her *Fuck Paintings*, Betty Tompkins unwittingly became part of a tradition of artists who preceded or worked alongside her. Carolee Schneemann was one of the first artists to portray her vision of sexual climax onscreen. This former painter made an autobiographical experimental film entitled *Fuses* (1964-67) which resensualised and embodied the moving image. The film alternates between close-ups of the erect penis of her lover and partner during these three years, the composer James Tenney, and tight-focus shots of penetration and Schneemann pleasuring herself. The celluloid is texturized with grattage effects and the addition of paint which enhance the sensation of arousal. Schneemann was well ahead of the curve in this respect and strove to create a kinaesthetic environment combining elements of theatre and film. This first experimental film, which amplified physical sensations, is a forerunner of sex-positive feminism as we know it today. Visionary and unintentionally programmatic, *Fuses* blazed the trail for other East Coast forms in the United States, while eliciting harsh judgments about its origins from critics and museum curators. Carolee Schneemann's work is not derived from expressionist painting, assemblage art or happenings, and certainly not from music or experimental filmmaking, although it draws inspiration from them. Like Betty Tompkins, Carolee Schneemann operates outside defined and established art scenes. Even now, Schneemann's experiments still set her apart; although she is a major figure in art history, the diversity of her work transcends the feminist aesthetic established in the 1970s.

Reading her work in the light of how it was received reveals how this difficult transition from pop art to conceptual art was amplified when she was swept aside by the emergence of feminist consciousness. Another artist who bore the full brunt of this tectonic instability was Hannah Wilke.

Between 1969 and 1975, performance artist Hannah Wilke produced a series of portraits of her partner, combining scenes of domesticity with moments of eroticism. This partner was none other than the artist Claes Oldenburg, a key pop art figure. However, Wilke depicts him fast asleep or vulnerable with a semi-erect penis – poses totally at odds with his reputation as a renowned artist. This series of photos was only exhibited once, in 1975, then relegated to a file in Wilke's archives under the heading "Men", which contained several hundred slides of her lovers. When the couple split, Oldenburg obtained a court order preventing the distribution of Wilke's photographic series, thus consigning the work to obscurity.[3] Hannah Wilke bore the full brunt of censorship of this photo-journal which was the fruit of several years' work, combining a pop art treatment of her subject with the focus on process characteristic of conceptual art. Contrary to all expectations, intimacy has experienced a revival in public life, decoupling Wilke from her feminist pop art work.

3 Tim Cone, 'Life Over Art: Oldenburg's privacy, Wilke's Publicity', *Arts Magazine* 64, No.1 (September 1989), pp.25-26.

This event earned her a place among a group of artists drawn together not by aesthetic affinities but by a desire to put an end to injustice. This collective launched a battle against the censorship of erotic/pornographic works made by women. The Fight Censorship group was founded in New York in 1973 by the figurative painter Anita Steckel, who was joined by Judith Bernstein, Louise Bourgeois, Martha Edelheit, Eunice Golden, Juanita McNeely, Barbara Nessim, Anne Sharpe, Joan Semmel, and Hannah Wilke.[4] By way of a manifesto, and to mark the widespread distribution of a leaflet on 8 March 1973, Steckel wrote:

4 Richard Meyer, "Hard Targets: Male Bodies, Feminist Art and the Force of Censorship in the 1970s" in *WACK! Art and the Feminist Revolution*, 2007-9, https://www.amherst.edu/ system/files/media/1098/Butler_ Hard_Targets_Male_Bodies.PDF

> "We women artists… We believe sexual subject matter should be removed from the 'closet' of the fine arts where it resides in small portfolios, small works, off the walls, in private collections, etc. […]. It is always the men who cover their sex, who hide what they consider 'their shame', who think of their sexuality as unwholesome […]. We women artists object to this unhealthy and sexist discrimination and we demand an end to past sexist puritanisms in museums. […] we demand that sexual subject matter, as it is part of life, no longer be prevented from being part of art. […] If the erect penis is not wholesome enough to go into museums it should not be considered wholesome enough to go into women. And if the erect penis is wholesome enough to go into women, then it is more than wholesome enough to go into the greatest art museums."[5]

5 https://www.brooklynmuseum.org/eascfa/about/feminist_art_base/anita-steckel

The Fight Censorship group made several public appearances on television, at art schools and on college campuses. During a lecture at the New York School for Social Research in October 1973, the artists adopted the unusual approach of appearing armed with their collages, sculptures and paintings, some of which were of a monumental scale. *Fillette*, an erect penis by Louise Bourgeois, was presented in this way, prior to being immortalised by Robert Mapplethorpe. The erect *Fillette* phallus was eventually cropped from the iconic portrait created for MoMA's Louise Bourgeois retrospective in 1982. Louise Bourgeois highlighted the absurdity of this reframing which excised the erotic aspect of her humour.[6] The history of the censorship of representations of visual pleasure embodied by women artists was inexorably repeating itself.

6 Mignon Nixon, *Fantastic Reality: Louise Bourgeois and a Story of Modern Art*, Cambridge, Massachusetts 2005, pp.71–81.

Like Louise Bourgeois, Anita Steckel and Judith Bernstein also chose to embrace priapic iconography, either by resorting to childish humour in the form of schoolgirl drawings of cocks on a landscape of Manhattan buildings against which giant women are pleasuring themselves in *New York Landscape* (1970-80) by Steckel, or by covering monumental paintings with screw-like penis machines – *Dicks* (1973) – in front of which Judith Bernstein staged a photograph of herself in a pose reminiscent of Betty Tompkins' portrait with her *Fuck Paintings*. This iconography was withdrawn from solo and group exhibitions such as *Woman's Work – America '74* at the Museum of the Philadelphia Civic Center. Curator Marcia Tucker dissociated herself from the project to mark her disapproval of the removal of Bernstein's paintings.[7]

7 Richard Meyer, "Hard Targets: Male Bodies, Feminist Art and the Force of Censorship in the 1970s" in *WACK! Art and the Feminist Revolution*, 2007-9, op. cit.

Censorship took different forms and operated at several levels – overtly, when the decency or morality argument was invoked and, more insidiously, when some feminists erased certain works in favour of others without making any attempt to defend their aesthetic choices. Examples include Cornelia Butler and Lisa Gabrielle Mark, curators of the seminal exhibition *WACK! Art and the Feminist Revolution* (2007), who removed from their list of artists several women working in the area of sexual politics – heterosexual and homosexual – or presenting scenes featuring male bodies. Radical North American feminism, informed by Marxist re-readings, has had a profound influence from the late 1960s to the present day on the way in which we consider certain works as feminist or non-feminist art. I firmly believe that this lies at the root of a number of misunderstandings and fundamental disagreements around representations of bodies and desires. However, this feminism was one of the trends structuring the concept of "sexual politics", long before the publication of Michel Foucault's *History of Sexuality*.

Sexual Politics: Feminism and Marxism, A Potent Partnership

We undoubtedly owe the political concept of (female) sex and sexualities (heterosexual and homosexual) to the feminist-Marxist theorist Kate Millett. In 1968, she published her first essay based on the premises of the Women's Liberation movement, precursor of her thesis entitled *Sexual Politics*. When this thesis was published in 1970, it was a bestseller in the United States and internationally. It was quickly translated into French and perfectly reflected the diverse early manifestations of the MLF, the French women's liberation movement. Millett's heuristic input consisted of redefining the notion of "politics/the political". In a marked departure from accepted models, this PhD student in comparative literature shifted the notion of power, interpreted as the oppressive operation of institutions in a pyramidal structure, towards the private sphere. In short, Kate Millett was responsible for making a connection between "politics/the political" and our bodies and subjectivities and thus developing the new paradigm that "the personal is political" which has been so fundamental from the birth of the women's liberation movement right through to contemporary "transfeminism".[8]

8 Interview with Sam Bourcier, « La révolution transféministe », episode 87, podcast *La Poudre*, https://podtail.com/podcast/la-poudre/episode-87-la-revolution-transfeministe-avec-sam-b/

The author of *Sexual Politics* was herself influenced conceptually and politically by the political actions and thinking of the civil rights movement which named and shamed the white supremacists who ruled – and still rule – in the United States on the basis of "one ancient and universal arrangement for the political exploitation of one birth group by another," according to Millett. By way of response, in 1968, Millett called on women "black and white" to organise themselves into a class to confront this policy of sexual domination. With great lucidity, Millett broke the long silence by asking: "Why, when this arrangement of male rule and control of our society is so obvious – why is it never acknowledged or discussed?"[9] Following on from this question, she drew attention to a blind spot which frequently occurs in the coarse, smutty guise of mockery: "Sex is funny – it's dirty – and it is something women have."[10] Men, by contrast are not "sexual beings", "they are humanity". According to this radical feminist, humanity is afflicted by a "conspiracy" organised along "folk myth" lines, which is in turn shaped by the myth of the devil woman. "The phantasy of the male victim" is not merely the stuff of legend, but a politically expedient argument against any attempt to question or, worse still, challenge this policy of sexual domination. This is framed in material terms as an attack on their sex by means of "castration". Moreover, Millett adds that this fear extends far beyond mere symbolism as it has motivated a large number of punitive actions by members of the Ku Klux Klan against African-American citizens.

9 Kate Millett, *Sexual Politics*, essay 1968: https://www.marxists.org/subject/women/authors/millett-kate/sexual-politics.htm

10 Idem.

Shulamith Firestone, another major figure of radical American feminism, took Millett's thinking a step further by advocating the establishment and recognition of women as a social class. Her innovative approach involved transposing the Marxist concept of the means of industrial production to sexual organs, which she identified as "tools" in the struggle. As a technophile, which was unusual among feminists, Firestone believed that scientific progress held the potential to free women from submission to reproduction and diminishment based on their
11 sex. In *The Dialectic of Sex* (1970)[11], she refered to technically and cybernetically-assisted methods of conception. Her antipatriarchal vision was based on the eradication of the nuclear family legitimised purely by blood ties, and posited a society based on the principles of "intentional community", guided by socialism. A pedagogical and aesthetic response to this East Coast radical feminist thinking came in the form of Womanhouse, established by the artists Judy Chicago and Myriam Shapiro at Fresno College, and more tangentially at CalArts (Los Angeles). Judy Chicago, who was heavily influenced by Firestone, undertook iconographic experiments focusing on "central core" imagery. The support group running Womanhouse, comprising students and teachers, created a database of visual cultures and works of art which privileged vulval forms – defined as "sex-positive" – over phallic forms, which were already ubiquitous. Based on this anthological collection, Judy Chicago, who had a close affinity with Anaïs Nin's Freudian writing on desire, encouraged her students to experiment with embodying "cunt art".

Shulamith Firestone, *The Dialectic of Sex*, New York, William Morrow & Co, 1970.

The screenprint *Red Flag* (1971) is an iconic example of this movement, in which Judy Chicago reproduces a frontal view of her crotch. We can see a closed fist in the pubic area pulling the string of a tampon, which is two-thirds withdrawn, revealing the menstrual blood it has absorbed. The title echoes the call to revolution advocated in radical feminist writings which was picked up by various women's liberation movements. The shade of the flag is superimposed on the colour of the menstrual blood, intimating an unprecedented change – a massive uprising which would transform patriarchal and capitalist societies into a universal feminist and socialist "global village" (Marshall McLuhan). Like the screenprint, the class of women established in this way would be working towards expunging phallic forms (symbolic, physical and political) which penetrate and dominate them. An entire intellectual and activist movement became convinced in this way that pornography not only had its roots in rape culture but actually fuelled it.

However, the sisterhood of the new so-called "feminist" political class did not see eye to eye on the sexual politics of representation

or racial issues. Heterosexual culture and the symbolism of penetration got a bad press, but they remained a key topic for certain feminists and a powerful source of appropriation and transgression. Artists such as Betty Tompkins, who chose this subject or motif, and the expression of desire for male bodies, were perceived by feminist colleagues as outsiders, or worse still as "social traitors" producing counterpropaganda. It was only a small step from theoretical rejection to curatorial indifference of certain works. The painter Joan Semmel recalls: "In the late seventies, my self-image series became very well-known, and included several paintings in which a male lover is also seen [...] Predictably, if I was asked to participate in a group exhibition, I was usually asked for
12 the *female* nude image (without a male partner)."[12]

12 Joan Semmel cited by Richard Meyer, "Hard Targets: Male Bodies, Feminist Art and the Force of Censorship in the 1970s" in *WACK! Art and the Feminist Revolution*, 2007-9, *op. cit.*

Feminist Pornography and Queerness: What AIDS Did For Us

In his essay "Hard Targets: Male Bodies, Feminist Art and The Force of Censorship in the 1970s", queer art historian Richard Meyer expresses his belief that the rejection or invisibility of pornographic art produced by women is linked to the censorship of gay imagery in the 1960s and 1970s. Meyer is a recognised expert on homophobia in art, and more particularly on the social panic triggered by an overlooked work by Andy
13 Warhol depicting homoerotic desire.[13] For the World's Fair in 1964, the young artist was offered a public commission for a work to cover the huge façade of the New York State Pavilion. Warhol chose to depict on a stretched silk screen the *Thirteen Most Wanted Men* in the New York City police files. The mural comprised 13 portraits of "wanted" men in the same style as the *Car Crash* and *Electric Chair* series and also the series featuring icons James Dean and Marilyn Monroe, whose lives were brutally cut short. The double meaning of the word "wanted" was clearly not lost on the organisers. On the mayor's orders, there was a huge blitz to shut down gay venues and censor "camp" films and events. For the entire duration of the fair, Warhol's installation was covered up by a layer of silver paint. He responded by producing the film *The Thirteen Most Beautiful Boys*, featuring Gerard Malanga. Following this event, the FBI opened a file on the artist's non-conformist sexuality. The story made headlines, but has now been completely forgotten. Richard Meyer is puzzled by this protracted silence in the writings of female historians and curators. He considers this early work by Andy Warhol to be a powerful political gesture which contradicts the apolitical label usually applied to the high priest of pop art.

13 Richard Meyer, *Outlaw Representation: Censorship and Homosexuality in Twentieth-Century American Art* (2002), New York, Echo Point Book & Media, 2019.

Four decades later, when the *WACK!* exhibition erased an entire corpus of works by women/feminist artists depicting desired

male bodies, Meyer attempted to understand the mechanisms of erasure and censorship potentially applied to gay and feminist pornography alike. He reappraised a genealogy of women artists who did not always share emotional connections or aesthetic affinities. This seminal contribution brought this repressed aspect of feminism to my attention. His analysis was already at odds with the dominant trends in "post-feminist" art historical writing
14 of the 2000s represented by Peggy Phelan, Helena Rickitt[14], and Amelia Jones, for example. His libertarian ethos alerted me to the dangers of preconceptions in an ontological definition of feminist art. This queer art historian's perspective on feminist pornography raised the hypothesis of a social sanction shared with queer visual culture and struck me as affirmatory and politically legitimate. Unfortunately, Meyer's conclusions on the subject disappoint as the connections he was seeking do not ultimately materialise. He writes: "I expected to find points of overlap between the feminist project of the Fight Censorship group and the efforts of gay and lesbian artists in the 1970s to overcome censorship of homoerotic imagery. As mentioned above, however, lesbianism was rarely overtly addressed within early 1970s feminist art collectives and programs. Male homoerotic art, meanwhile, was typically seen by feminist critics of the day as
15 a sign of male privilege and female erasure."[15]

14 Helena Rickitt and Peggy Phelan, *Art and Feminism*, New York, Phaidon, 2006; Amelia Jones, *The Feminism and Visual Culture Reader*, New York, Routledge, 2002.

15 Richard Meyer, "Hard Targets: Male Bodies, Feminist Art and the Force of Censorship in the 1970s" in *WACK! Art and the Feminist Revolution*, 2007-9, op. cit.

This condemnation of gay pornography by Marxist feminism revealed a difficulty with thinking sexualities from a non-heterosexual perspective. Works by the Fight Censorship group and other queer art groups did not converge in the 1970s, as it was still too early. This history of affinities between the sex-positive vision of feminists and the need for sexual representations from different queer communities was accelerated
16 by the AIDS epidemic. In her essay on the Akimbo collective[16], Isabelle Alfonsi makes a powerful case for reclaiming public spaces through flyposting. In direct action initiatives at street level, pornographic images of diverse queer sexualities entitled simply "Just Sex", "Sex is" and "Safe" were posted by Act Up activists in San Francisco calling themselves Akimbo. This organisation was clearly acting in response to the censorship in 1989 of an exhibition of Robert Mapplethorpe's *X Portfolio* at the Corcoran Museum and the stigmatisation of cruising joints and sex parties by conservatives weaponizing the AIDS epidemic. This awareness of the urgent need to disseminate a porn imaginary that was joyful and celebratory in urban public spaces and art venues – a vision shared by Gran Fury in New York – was, moreover, accompanied by the rediscovery of a significant sex-positive corpus from the 1960s and 1970s which had been invalidated, as it were, by a group of Lacanian Marxist feminists running the British

16 Isabelle Alfonsi, *Pour une esthétique de l'émancipation*, Paris, B42, 2019.

visual culture magazine *Screen* in the mid-1970s, who developed an editorial policy around the destruction of the subject "woman". Sex-positive depictions of bodies were lambasted at the time for their "regressive", "neo-patriarchal" and "neo-capitalist" visions. According to art historian Griselda Pollock and the artist Mary Kelly, who spearheaded this "constructivist" battle against "essentialism", this free expression of subjectivities was merely a mechanical extension of the motto "the personal is political". Heavily influenced by Althusserian philosophy and Lacanian theory – to have or not to have a phallus – these two hard-line representatives of the British feminist movement were so focused on deconstructing the subject that they omitted to offer libertarian alternatives: the desiring utopias, so necessary in the context of the backlash in 1980s America and in the present day.

The rediscovery of a libertarian history of bodies, and its fertile iconography from a particular period – the transition from pop art to conceptual art – coincided and, I believe, continues to coincide with specific political circumstances. Whether it be in the years 1990-2000, as a reaction against an American conservative regime promoting neo-fascist positions and weaponizing the AIDS epidemic, or in the 2020s with the global spread of supremacist, ultra-liberal, and patriarchal ideologies, sex-positive feminist and queer imaginaries have come together and are still coming together to wage war. Were it not for the AIDS epidemic and the battles which it prompted, I firmly believe that we would not have access to many of the works and artists which Hélène Guenin and I rediscovered when we were carrying out research for the exhibition *Les Amazones du pop*.[17] We might not even have been in a position to re-evaluate them.

Looking at the *Fuck Paintings* today offers us a black box, the intangible memory of a process of invisibilization, which was motivated at the time, for diametrically opposed reasons, by conservative morals and feminist opprobrium. In both instances, these prejudices prompted harsh social and aesthetic sanctions against the artists involved. The "perverse" aspect of Tompkins' paintings shattered the entire historical and cultural construct of implicit and explicit censorship, and we are now witnessing this legacy today.

17 Cf. The exhibition catalogue for *Les Amazones du pop*, MAMAC, 2020-2022, ed. Géraldine Gourbe and Hélène Guenin, Paris, Flammarion, 2020.

PUSSY PAINTINGS

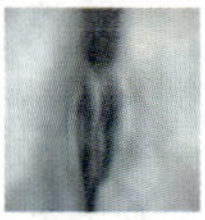
Pussy Painting #18
2012
Acrylic on canvas
40,6 × 40,6 cm
16 x 16 inches

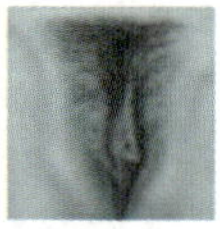
Pussy Painting #20
2012
Acrylic on canvas
40,6 × 40,6 cm
16 × 16 inches

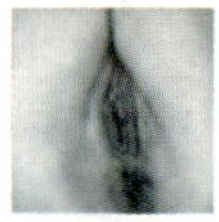
Pussy Painting #22
2012
Acrylic on canvas
40,6 × 40,6 cm
16 × 16 inches

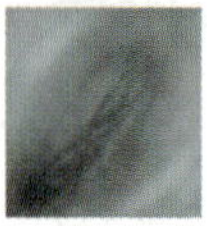
Pussy Painting #25
2013
Acrylic on canvas
40,6 × 40,6 cm
16 × 16 inches

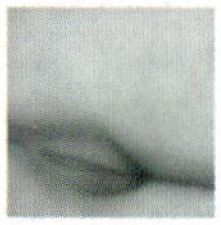
Pussy Painting #27
2016
Acrylic on canvas
40,6 × 40,6 cm
16 × 16 inches

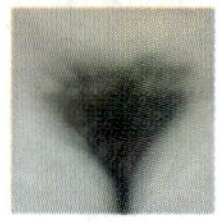
Pussy Painting #30
2017
Acrylique sur toile
Acrylic on canvas
40,6 × 40,6 cm
16 × 16 inches

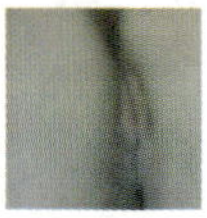
Pussy Painting #32
2017
Acrylic on canvas
40,6 × 40,6 cm
16 × 16 inches

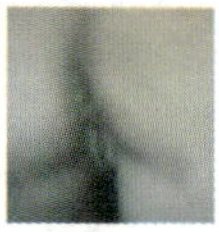
Pussy Painting #33
2017
Acrylic on canvas
40,6 × 40,6 cm
16 × 16 inches

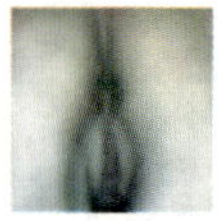
Pussy Painting #34
2017
Acrylic on canvas
40,6 × 40,6 cm
16 × 16 inches

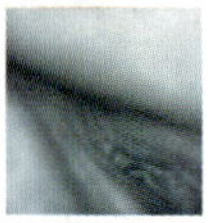
Pussy Painting #23
2013
Acrylic on canvas
40,6 × 40,6 cm
16 × 16 inches

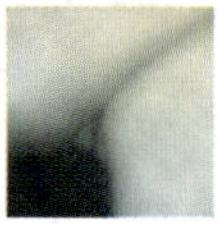
Pussy Painting #31
2017
Acrylic on canvas
40,6 × 40,6 cm
16 × 16 inches

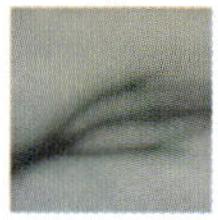
Pussy Painting #35
2017
Acrylic on canvas
40,6 × 40,6 cm
16 × 16 inches

FUCK PAINTINGS

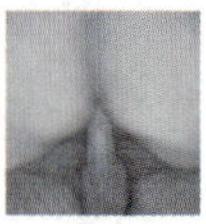
Fuck Painting #47
2012
Acrylic on canvas
182,88 × 182,88 cm
72 × 72 inches

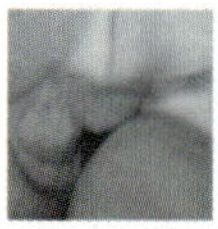
Fuck Painting #54
2016
Acrylic on canvas
162,6 × 162,6 cm
64 × 64 inches

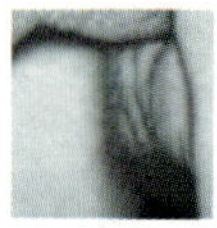
Fuck painting #59
2017
Acrylic on canvas
152,4 × 147,3 cm
60 × 58 inches

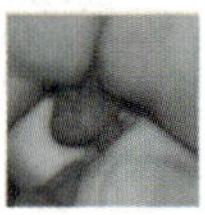
Fuck Painting #50
2014
Acrylic on canvas
147,32 × 152,4 cm
58 × 60 inches

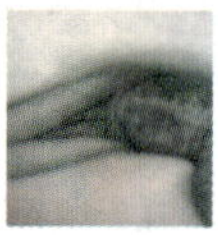
Fuck Painting #60
2019
Acrylic on canvas
152,4 × 147,3 cm
60 × 58 inches

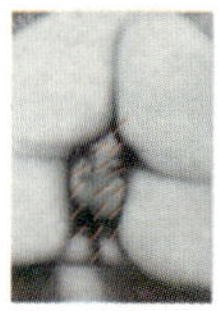
Censored Painting #2
(Paris 1973 - Instagram 2019)
2019
Acrylic on canvas
213,4 × 152,4 cm
84 × 60 inches

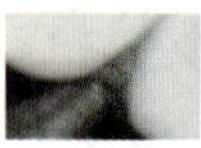
Fuck Painting #53
2015
Acrylic on canvas
55,88 × 91,44 cm
22 × 36 inches

INSULTS AND LAMENTS

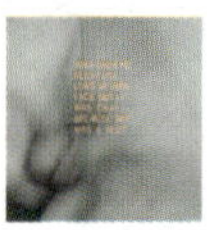
And then he...
2018
Acrylic on canvas
61 × 61 cm
24 × 24 inches

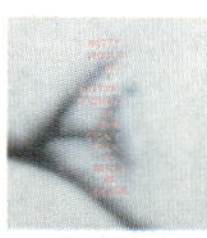
Betty would...
2018
Acrylic on canvas
61 × 61 cm
24 × 24 inches

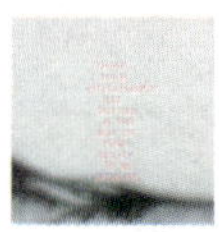
I think...
2018
Acrylic on canvas
61 × 61 cm
24 × 24 inches

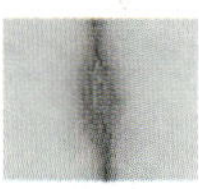
My ex's favorite...
2018
Acrylic on canvas
106,7 × 137,2 cm
42 × 54 inches

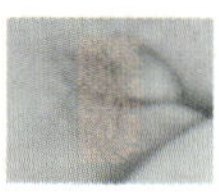
Poopsie...
2018
Acrylic on canvas
106,7 × 137,2 cm
42 × 54 inches

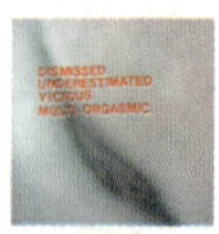
Dismissed...
2015
Acrylic on canvas
45,7 × 45,7 cm
18 × 18 inches

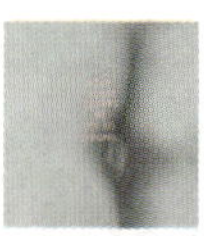
Your pussy...
2018
Acrylic on canvas
61 × 61 cm
24 × 24 inches

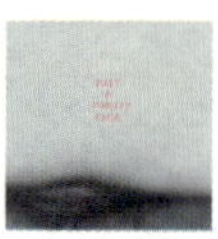
Just a Pretty Face
2019
Acrylic on canvas
61 × 86,4 cm
24 × 34 inches

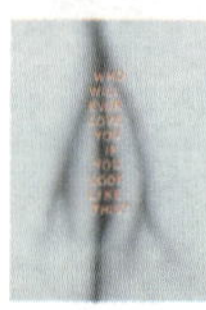
Who will...
2019
Acrylic on canvas
61 × 45,7 cm
24 × 18 inches

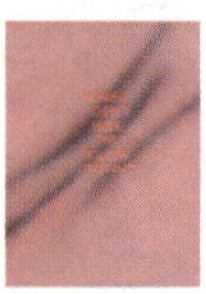
Women Don't Have Killer Instinct
2019
Acrylic on canvas
61 × 45,7 cm
24 × 18 inches

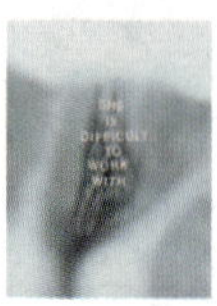
She is...
2018
Acrylic on canvas
61 × 45,7 cm
24 × 18 inches

CUNT PAINTINGS

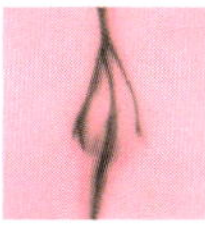

Cunt Painting #29
2017
Acrylic on canvas
61 × 61 cm
24 × 24 inches

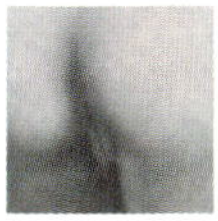

Cunt Painting #31
2018
Acrylique sur toile
Acrylic on canvas
162,6 × 162,6 cm
64 × 64 inches

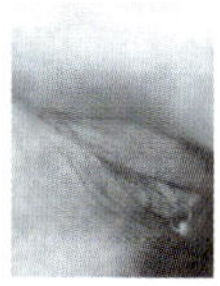

Cunt Painting #16
2011
Acrylique sur toile
Acrylic on canvas
137.2 x 106.7 cm
54 × 42 inches

COLLAGES

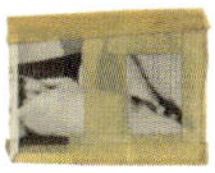

Collage #2
1970
Mixed media
7 × 8,9 cm
2 ¾ × 3 ½ inches

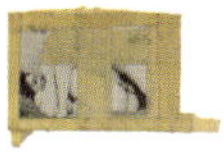

Collage #3
1970
Mixed media
7,6 × 15,24 cm
3 × 6 inches

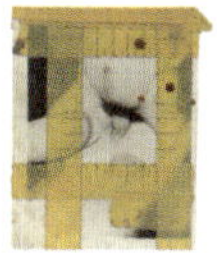

Collage #4
1973
Mixed media
12,7 × 11,4 cm
5 × 4 ½ inches

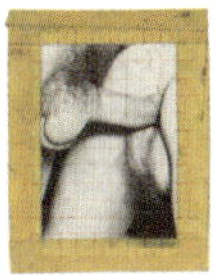

Collage #6
1973
Mixed media
12,7 × 10,2 cm
5 × 4 inches

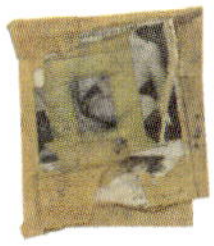

Collage #8 and *Collage #9*
1974
Mixed media
15,2 × 13,3 cm
6 × 5,2 inches

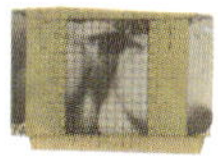

Collage #11
1976
Mixed media
18,4 × 11,4 cm
7,25 × 4 ½ inches

GRID DRAWINGS AND PAINTINGS

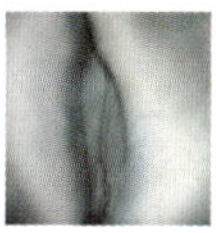

Cunt Grid Painting #3
2016
Acrylic and pencil on paper
74,9 × 105,4 cm
29 ½ × 41 ½ inches

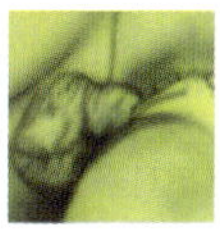

Fuck Grid Painting #6
2016
Acrylic and pencil on paper
74,9 × 105,4 cm
29 ½ × 41 ½ inches

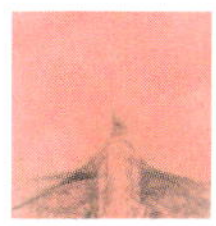

Fuck Grid #55
2017
Pencil and colored pencil on paper
43,2 × 35,6 cm
17 × 14 inches

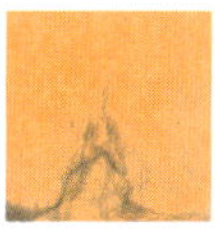

Fuck Grid #56
2017
Pencil and colored pencil on paper
43,2 × 35,6 cm
17 × 14 inches

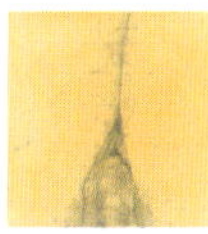

Fuck Grid #57
2017
Pencil and colored pencil on paper
43,2 × 35,6 cm
17 × 14 inches

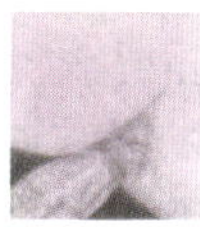

Fuck Grid #53
2017
Pencil and colored pencil on paper
43,2 × 35,6 cm
17 × 14 inches

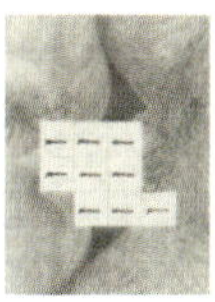

Censored Grid #10
[Grille censurée]
2008
Pencil and ink on paper
43,2 × 35,6 cm
17 × 14 inches

Cunt Grid Painting #2
2016
Acrylic and pencil on paper
74,9 × 105,4 cm
29 ½ × 41 ½ inches

PHOTO DRAWINGS

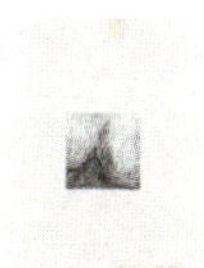

Photo Drawing #10
2014
Mixed media
27,9 × 21,6 cm
11 × 8 ½ inches

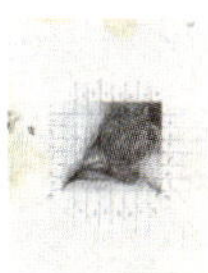

Photo Drawing #19
2014
Mixed media
27,9 × 21,6 cm
11 × 8 ½ inches

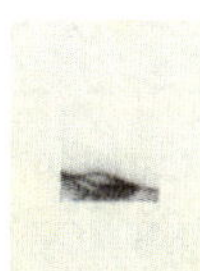

Photo Drawing #6
2014
Mixed media
27,9 × 21,6 cm
11 × 8 ½ inches

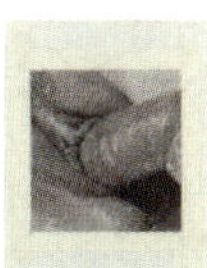

Photo Drawing #8
2014
Mixed media
27,9 × 21,6 cm
11 × 8 ½ inches

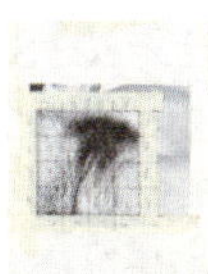

Photo Drawing #13
2014
Mixed media
27,9 × 21,6 cm
11 × 8 ½ inches

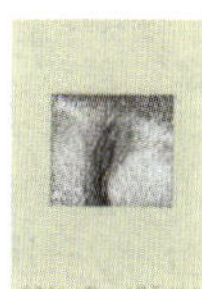

Photo Drawing #5
2014
Mixed media
27,9 × 21,6 cm
11 × 8 ½ inches

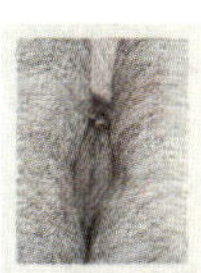

Photo Drawing #7
2014
Mixed media
27,9 × 21,6 cm
11 × 8 ½ inches

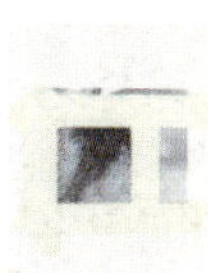

Photo Drawing #21
2014
Mixed media
27,9 × 21,6 cm
11 × 8 ½ inches

ALISON M. GINGERAS

A curator and writer, Alison M. Gingeras has been recognized for her scholarly yet anarchic approach to art history. She has held curatorial positions at the Solomon R. Guggenheim Museum, New York, the Centre Pompidou, Paris, and Francois Pinault's Palazzo Grassi, Venice. Gingeras serves as Adjunct Curator of Dallas Contemporary and Guest Curator of the Museum of Contemporary Art North Miami. She has organized groundbreaking exhibitions such as *Black Sheep Feminism (The Art of Sexual Politics)* (2016) and *Sex Work: Feminist Art & Radical Politics* (2017) at Frieze London. Her essays regularly appear in periodicals including *Artforum, Spike, Mousse, Playboy,* and *Tate Etc.*, and in scores of art historical volumes.

GÉRALDINE GOURBE

Géraldine Gourbe is a philosopher, art critic and curator. She has taught Philosophy of Art and is a specialist on inclusive feminism. In 2018, she curated an exhibition on the work of Judy Chicago and the West Coast in the 1960s, *Los Angeles, The Cool Years* (Villa Arson). Since 2015, she has been developing a counter-reading of the history of ideas and art in France from 1947 to 1989. This research has led to the organisation of the exhibition *Gigantism* (Dunkirk Art and esign Triennial). In 2020, she co-curated with Hélène Guenin *She Bam Pow POP Wizz : Les Amazones du Pop* (MAMAC Nice). She has published a monograph on the artist Judy Chicago, *To Sustain the Vision* (Shelter Press, Rennes: March 2020), and has just published an essay on Simone de Beauvoir.

ANYA HARRISON

Anya Harrison is curator at MO.CO. Montpellier Contemporain where she works on developing exhibition projects, the live art programme and publications. Previously, she was a member of the Baltic Triennial 13 curatorial team (2017-2018) and was Assistant Curator for the Pavilion of Kosovo at the 58th Venice Biennale (2019). Independent co-curated projects include *The Return of Memory* (HOME, Manchester, 2017), *Ceremony* with Phil Collins (Manchester International Festival, 2017) and New East Cinema (ICA, Calvert 22 and the Barbican, London, 2014-2017). As an independent art critic and writer, she has contributed to publications including *Frieze, Artforum, CURA* and *Flash Art International*, and exhibition catalogues.

BETTY TOMPKINS

Since the late 1960s, Betty Tompkins (b. 1945, Washington, D.C., USA) has engaged with a sexually explicit iconography. Two paintings from her first series of *Fuck Paintings* (1969-1974) were refused entry to France in 1973, stopped at customs and confiscated due to their content, which was deemed pornographic in nature. The *Fuck Paintings* were not shown until 2002, when Tompkins had her first solo exhibition at Mitchell Algus Gallery, the New York gallerist who (re)discovered her. Tompkins' work was finally shown in France in 2003 at the Lyon Biennale, and the following year *Fuck Painting #1* entered the permanent collection of the Centre Pompidou in Paris.

Her work has been presented in exhibitions in Kunstraum Innsbruck, FLAG Art Foundation (New York), Confort Moderne (Poitiers), Villa Arson (Nice), Dallas Contemporary (Texas) and the Centre Pompidou, Musée d'art moderne (Paris), among others.

CATALOGUE

Editorial Direction:
David Desrimais & Mathieu Cénac, assisted by Samantha Calteau, JBE Books
Anya Harrison, MO.CO.

Graphic Design:
Joanna Starck

Textes:
Nicolas Bourriaud
Alison M. Gingeras
Géraldine Gourbe
Anya Harrison

Translation:
Denyse Beaulieu
Maxime Brousse
Clara Muller
CG Traduction

Proofreading:
Rahmouna Boutayeb
Pauline Faure
Anya Harrison
Emma Ribeyre

Photo Credits:
Courtesy of Betty Tompkins, P·P·O·W, New York and rodolphe janssen, Brussels

Cunt Painting #16,
Fuck Painting #59
and *Fuck Grid #53*:
photo Credit HV photography
© Betty Tompkins

Colour Correction:
IGS Print

Paper:
Arctic Volume White
Munken Pure

Typefaces:
Aktiv Grotesk © Dalton Maag
Kandal © Mark Simonson Studio

Distribution:
D.A.P. Artbook
(North America, Latin America, Asia)
Antenne Books (United Kingdom)
Interart (France)
Vice Versa Distribution (Germany)

ISBN 978-2-36568-040-0

EXHIBITION

This catalogue is published on the occasion of the exhibition *Betty Tompkins: Raw Material*

MO.CO. Panacée
26 June – 5 September 2021

Under the artistic direction of Nicolas Bourriaud

Curators:
Vincent Honoré, Head of Exhibitions
Anya Harrison, Curator
Rahmouna Boutayeb, Project Manager

Assisted by:
Fanny Hugot-Conte, Emma Ribeyre and Justine Vic

Graphic Design (Historical Timeline):
Johanna Himmelsbach, Kai Udema

Acknowledgements:
Wendy Olsoff, Penny Pilkington, Jennifer Brennan and the team from P·P·O·W, New York

Rodolphe Janssen, Victoria Grolaux and the team from rodolphe janssen, Brussels

Betty Tompkins wishes to extend her thanks to all of the individuals and teams mentioned above, as well as Anya Harrison, Vincent Honoré and to Alison M. Gingeras and Géraldine Gourbe for their catalogue essays.

The exhibition *Betty Tompkins: Raw Material* is organised with the support of P·P·O·W, New York

MO.CO. MONTPELLIER CONTEMPORAIN

Chief Executive Officer:
Nicolas Bourriaud

Head of Exhibitions:
Vincent Honoré

Director of MO.CO. ESBA – Ecole supérieure des Beaux-Arts:
Yann Mazéas

Administrative Director:
Julien Fournel

General Coordination and Partnerships:
Delphine Goutes

Curatorial Team:
Caroline Chabrand, Pauline Faure, Anya Harrison, Anna Kerekes, Victor Secretan

Project Manager:
Rahmouna Boutayeb

Collections Project Manager:
Gwendoline Corthier-Hardoin

Administration:
Marc Choinard, Françoise Tilly

Human Resources:
Géraldine Siedel

Communications:
Margaux Strazzeri, Sémiha Cebti, Adeline Touraut

Technical Management and Team:
Pierre Bellemin, Maurice Schmitt, Jean-Adrien Arzilier, Christophe Blanc, Patricia Gloria, Thomas Bertetti

Installation Team:
Frédéric Brisset, Luc Castanié, Amandine Contat, Pierre-Guilhem Coste, Christophe Dansard, Eric Dupin, Bruno Ferrier, Marie Havel, Anouk Lepeigneul, Reno Leplat-Torti, Marion Lisch, Marilou Martinez, Karine Secretant, Thomas Pelet, Clément Philippe

Education Department:
Stéphanie Delpeuch, Fanny Berquière, Charlotte Winling, Pascale Battistelli, Corinne Gèrent, Emeline Sivadier

Gallery Guides and Mediators:
Marie Boutevin, Jeanine Lasjaunias, Guilhem Morand, Marie-Cécile Perez, Céline Pires, Lucile Ramirez-Thiers, Agathe Vial

MO.CO.MONTPELLIER CONTEMPORAIN

EPCC MO.CO. is supported by the Ville de Montpellier, Montpellier Métropole Méditerranée and the Direction Régionale des Affaires Culturelles Occitanie.

Montpellier Contemporain (MO.CO.) is an artistic ecosystem, ranging from practical training through to academic research. The model encompasses an arts school and two exhibition centres: MO.CO. ESBA (Montpellier Art School), MO.CO. Panacée (Contemporary Arts Centre) and, since June 2019, MO.CO. Hôtel des collections, an exhibition centre dedicated to public and private international collections.

Jean Boîte Éditions
51 rue Claude Decaen,
F-75012 Paris
jbe-books.com

Legal deposit: June 2021
First edition

Printed in Lithuania